SOCIAL
MEDIA
MADE EASY

This is a FLAME TREE book
First published 2013

Publisher and Creative Director: Nick Wells
Project Editor: Polly Prior
Art Director and Layout Design: Mike Spender
Digital Design and Production: Chris Herbert
Copy Editor: Anna Groves
Screenshots: Roger Laing

This edition first published 2013 by
FLAME TREE PUBLISHING
Crabtree Hall, Crabtree Lane
Fulham, London SW6 6TY
United Kingdom

www.flametreepublishing.com

13 15 17 16 14
1 3 5 7 9 10 8 6 4 2

© 2013 Flame Tree Publishing Ltd

ISBN 978-0-85775-625-1

A CIP record for this book is available from the British Library upon request.

Printed in China

All non-screenshot pictures are courtesy of Shutterstock and © the following photographers: tovovan 1; David Hammonds 3; Photosani 4 & 14; ra2 studio 5t & 46, 6b & 180; Vima 5b & 92; Hasloo Group Production Studio 6t & 136; Kurhan 7 & 224.

SOCIAL MEDIA
MADE EASY

ROGER LAING

**FLAME TREE
PUBLISHING**

CONTENTS

If you're new to social media then this is the place to start. This chapter explains what social media is and what you can do with it. It also describes the different types of social media, guiding you through the various sites and applications around. There is valuable information on how to set up an account, how to stay safe online and how to avoid copyright problems, plus what you'll need to get going. Finally, it lists the major dos and don'ts.

SOCIAL NETWORKS

Social networks are the most popular type of social media, especially thanks to sites like Facebook. This chapter features a detailed guide to Facebook with step-by-step instructions on how to set up an account, link up with your friends and family, upload photos and videos and much more. With plenty of tips on how to use LinkedIn to promote your career, here you can also discover Google+, the latest social network set to rival Facebook.

BLOGGING

Blogging is a great way to share your thoughts with the world and it has never been easier to do. This chapter reveals all about the blogosphere and will show you how to become one of the new social commentators. You'll find lots of information on Twitter – easily the best-known microblogging site there is – and how to use it. You'll also learn how to start your own blog and how to use forums, the original social media.

Whether you want to show your friends your holiday snaps or send your video viral then this chapter can help. Guiding you through the online communities that focus on sharing, it provides clear instructions on how to share your videos on YouTube and your interests on Pinterest, the latest social networking phenomenon. There is a section on how to use Tumblr to share things in an instant, plus you'll also find out how to share your photos on Flickr and your writing on Wikis.

For all you budding Richard Bransons out there, this chapter will show you how to promote your business through social media. Here you'll find step-by-step instructions on how to build your company's profile, including how to advertise on social networking sites like Facebook and LinkedIn. You'll also find advice on how to use Twitter to develop your brand, as well as vital information on how to build a following and how to stay ahead of your competitors.

FURTHERING YOUR SOCIAL NETWORK

Are you ready to take things further? The final chapter of this book looks at the range of special interest social media sites available – everything from social news sites (like Digg), social bookmarking sites (like Delicious) and social review sites (like Epinions), to music sharing sites (like Spotify), location-sharing sites (like Foursquare), video sharing sites (like Vimeo) and shared-interest communities. It also introduces you to virtual gaming sites (like Farmville) and virtual worlds (like Second Life).

INTRODUCTION

Social media is here to stay. If you doubt it, look at any magazine or newspaper article, listen to radio programmes, watch adverts on TV and you'll usually see some link to a Facebook page, Twitter account or blog. The conversation is in full flow and waiting for you to join in.

EVERYTHING YOU NEED TO KNOW

Social media is no longer new. It has been around in various forms since 2003, but it does move fast and new ways of communicating and connecting with people, whether they live on the other side of the world or next door, are evolving all the time. Social media is all about communicating, and most sites are user-friendly and designed to get you involved straight away. Inevitably, though, like all communities and groups of people with shared interests, there's a common language that develops, which can seem strange at first.

Above: Microblogging website Twitter allows you to connect with and follow like-minded groups, communities and individuals.

The result is that social media sites often have different names for similar activities. So writing a post on your blog is similar to updating your status on Facebook, or even sending a tweet on Twitter. Don't worry: this book will guide you through the jargon to explain simply and clearly what each phrase means. For a handy reference, you can refer to the Jargon Buster at the back of the book.

GO SOCIAL, WHEREVER YOU ARE

The range of social media is immense. While you are probably familiar with a few, such as Facebook, Twitter, LinkedIn and the like, there are literally thousands more. Whatever your interest – political debate, Baroque architecture, making muffins or stand-up comedy – there is a network, community, forum or group of people that will share it. There is so much choice, it can be quite bewildering to know where to start and how to get involved.

This book will help you find your way through the social media landscape. It will guide you through the range of social media, from social networks and forums to blogs and video- or photo-sharing sites – for both personal and business use. You will also see how easy it is to access the social world online from your computer, smartphone or tablet.

Above: You won't be on your own with this book – we will guide you through the social-media jungle step by step.

BITE-SIZE INFORMATION

When you join in a conversation or read a post on a social media site, you'll pretty soon find that you've followed a link that's taken you elsewhere. You can browse this book in the same way. You can read it, page by page, so that by the end you'll have total mastery of social media! However, you'll find it just as useful as a handy guide that you can dip into to discover the different tools that social media offers and how they can help you organize your life – and business.

For that reason, it's written in short, stand-alone sections. It includes several simple guides for tasks you can try for yourself. For example, you can find out how to use video to promote your business through social media. You'll also find a handy reference that shows you how to upload your video to YouTube and how to tweak the settings for perfect playback.

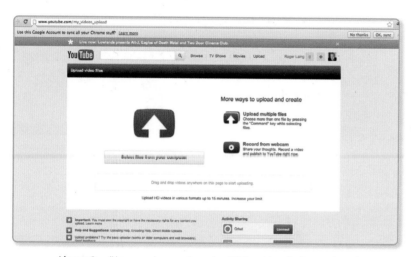

Above: It will be easy when you know how! This guide will take you through actions, such as uploading video, step-by-step.

STEP BY STEP

Throughout this book you'll find there are many step-by-step guides that take you through the exact actions you need to follow to accomplish certain tasks. This may be anything from opening an account on Twitter to managing the privacy settings on a photo-sharing site. Each step-by-step guide has clear, concise instructions on what to do as well as Hot Tips that will help you get the most from your social media tools – and have fun along the way.

HELP!

In the unlikely event you get really stuck on a particular topic, we're here to help. Simply email your query to Flame Tree Publishing at support@flametreepublishing.com. While we cannot operate a 24-hour helpline to cover the tremendous range of social media available, we will respond by email as soon as possible.

YOUR GUIDE

If you are new to blogs, Facebook, Twitter and the like, this book is designed to get you up and running as quickly as possible. Social media is designed to be open to all, so even if your computer experience is limited to browsing the web, you'll soon feel at ease. There's plenty too for the more experienced user. The author Roger Laing will introduce you to a much broader range of social media than you are likely to meet elsewhere. He'll explain briefly and clearly the range of social media you can use to connect and communicate with people, organize your life, and promote yourself and your business. Above all, by giving you a deeper understanding of how to use social media tools, he'll help you enjoy the experience.

DO MORE

Social media is an umbrella term that covers a vast range of online activities. They are social in the sense that they involve communities of people who share similar interests, with the users generating the content. Everyone is likely to have their favourites. You may like the immediacy of Twitter, where reaction to breaking events is instant. You may prefer only to share your activities with selected friends and family, such as on Facebook.

Alternatively, if you're seeking a wider audience, you may want your blog to be read around the world, promoted through sites like Blogger; or share your photos with fellow enthusiasts in your own gallery on Flickr. The good thing is you don't have to choose between any of these. All these and many more are waiting for you to get involved. This book will get you started; after that, the possibilities are virtually unlimited.

Above: StumbleUpon recommends sites and links to you according to your interests, helping you get a richer online experience.

SIX CHAPTERS

The contents of this book are split into six chapters. Chapter One will show you how to get started with social media and the many web-based sites and applications available. It also explains the dos and don'ts of social media. Chapter Two covers social networks, including Facebook, LinkedIn and Google+. Chapter Three is all about the blogosphere. It shows you how to start your own blog, as either a hosted or self-hosted site. For writing short blog posts, it also introduces the most famous microblogging site of them all – Twitter – and shows you how to get started. Chapter Four is all about sharing. Learn how to share videos on YouTube, photos on Flickr, interests on Pinterest, content on Tumblr, or writing on Wikis. For you entrepreneurs wanting to promote your business on social media, chapter Five will show you how.

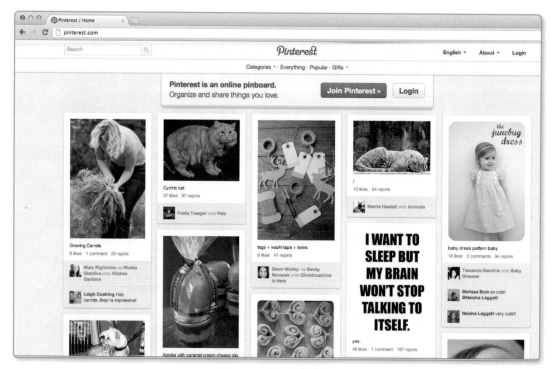

Above: Pinterest is the place to post info about all the things you love so that others can learn to love them too.

Chapter Six is your guide to the rich variety of special-interest social media sites available – ranging from social news (such as Digg), social bookmarking (Delicious) and social review sites (Trip Advisor), to music sharing (Myspace, Spotify) and the newer location-based social networks (Foursquare). It also looks at virtual gaming sites, with social games like Farmville that you can play with friends across the world, as well as the new social personas you can adopt in virtual worlds, such as Second Life.

Above: Social media can also help you to connect with others in virtual worlds, such as Second Life.

HOT TIPS AND SHORTCUTS

Look out for Hot Tips throughout the book, which provide quick and handy information on the way to get the best from your social media. They also highlight many shortcuts and quick techniques, which will help you become an expert user.

JARGON BUSTER!

Here in one handy list are simple explanations to de-mystify some of the social media terms and phrases you'll come across, from avatars to widgets.

GETTING STARTED

WHAT IS SOCIAL MEDIA?

We are by nature social animals. Social media builds on that instinct by enabling us to connect and share with people. It may be our ideas, news, photos, videos or opinions – anything and everything about our life that we want to let others know about.

WHAT SOCIAL MEDIA COVERS

Social media has become the way to communicate information between people, wherever they are. It is, in fact, an umbrella term that covers any website that connects people and shares information. As such, it describes much of the Internet. Under that umbrella, though, there are services that have built up an enormous following and turned social media into mass media. These include:

- **Social networks**: like Facebook (facebook.com), the original and best-known, or like LinkedIn (www.linkedin.com), used by professionals for networking

- **Blogs**: online journals for individuals and businesses

- **Microblogs**: such as Twitter (twitter.com), used for short, instant blogging

- **Video and photo sharing**: YouTube (www.youtube.com), Flickr (www.flickr.com)

- **Other sites**: Including social bookmarking, news sites, online reviews, music networks, social games and virtual worlds.

Hot Tip

Most newspapers and broadcasters run blog sites, written by their staff, to which you can add comments. Try these out for yourself and get used to how they work before you launch your own blog.

What distinguishes them all is that you – and the other people in the community – are actively involved in generating the content.

Unlike traditional media (TV, radio, etc.), communication is two-way. You write the blog, make the video or recommend a travel destination, and others can comment on it and make their own suggestions. Even if the source of the original content was a news site, or some other form of traditional media, it is still interactive – you can add your voice to it, comment or give feedback and create something new. What's more, it can all happen instantly.

Above: Most of the traditional print media are now online and actively encourage readers to comment on their stories.

A FAST-MOVING PHENOMENON

New forms of social media evolve and take off very quickly. Until recently, few would have thought that creating a pinboard of things you like would become an online phenomenon, yet Pinterest (pinterest.com) has. It is hard to define. Some call it a photo-sharing site, a bookmarking site, a pinboard, magazine and so on. Whatever it is, it is currently among the top three most-visited social media platforms. How Pinterest is viewed also varies between cultures. In the US, it is mainly used by women for fashion and crafts. By contrast, in Europe there are more male than female users and it is often used for business presentations.

WHAT YOU CAN DO WITH SOCIAL MEDIA

Typically, the collection of online services for publishing and sharing content that is called social media can help you:

- **Communicate with people you know:** Many social networks, like Facebook, start from the premise that you connect first with the people you know. This is usually done by checking your contacts' addresses against those of existing members of the site. After all, it is natural that you would want to share updates about what is going on in your life with family and friends.

- **Find new people to communicate with:** Once you have an established network, it is then easier to extend this to include friends of friends. You will see their news shared by your friends and you can add them as a friend. Equally, you can move outside of your existing circle by following an event – such as a music festival or book launch – or joining a group and meeting new people who share your interests.

- **Find people you've lost touch with:** Among the early social networks were several that specifically aimed to reunite people who had lost touch. Sites like Classmates in the US enable you to look for friends from your high-school days. A similar site in the UK, Friends Reunited, also lets you locate school, university or workplace friends. Recently, it

Above: Sites such as Friends Reunited now allow you to share memories of people and places.

has widened its scope so you can also search for photos and videos of events, places and great national moments, such as the 1966 World Cup final. Press the Keep button and you can save the item to your personal memory box.

⊙ **Find or set up a group**: Fascinated by vampires? There may not be many in your immediate area who share the same interest but there are plenty online. In fact, the social network Vampire Freaks (www.vampirefreaks.com) has more than 1.5 million members. Whatever your interest, there is likely to be a group that you can join. If not, it's easy to start your own, whether it's a Biffy Clyro fan page on Facebook or a professional group for ethical entrepreneurs on LinkedIn.

⊙ **Keep in touch with what's going on**: The joy of social media is that it helps you to keep track of personal news of friends and family, alongside receiving updates on your other interests. Through the same sites you can find out the latest world news, when your favourite band is on tour, the big trends in your industry, new techniques for night photography, injury news about your team, Madonna's favourite spa water or your friends' plan to renovate their house.

Hot Tip

Because of its huge membership base, Facebook is a good place to create an active group. It is easily done by setting up a Fan Page.

Above: The internet allows those with particularly specialized interests to connect with each other.

ORGANIZE EVERYDAY LIFE

Some avoid social media for fear that it is too distracting and will take up all their time. In fact, rather than being excessively time-consuming, social media can help you organize your time and live life to the full.

ORGANIZE YOUR SOCIAL LIFE

Arranging an evening out? This is when sites like Facebook come into their own. Easily accessed by computer at home or work, or through your mobile on the go, it's the perfect way for a network of friends to stay in touch. If someone's running late, or there's a change of venue, it's easier to post details on Facebook, where everyone can see, rather than phone people individually and get them to pass on a message.

Entertainment

There is so much going on, at the theatre, on the TV, in the cinema, how do you decide what to go and see? Previously, you might have read a review by a newspaper critic to help you make the

choice. You still can, but now you are also able to read what all the critics say in one place. In addition, you can see other users' comments on their views. You can access entertainment forums and view the ratings and comments that others have given. Or you can go by the advice of a friend, whose opinion you value, even though you haven't talked to them recently. How? Simple, just read their comments on Twitter.

Above: Sites like Rotten Tomatoes have all the critics' reviews in one place to help you decide if you want to see a film or not.

Events

It's difficult enough to arrange a party, particularly a surprise party, when everyone involved is in the same house. Imagine then, if those you want to invite are scattered all over the country, or even living in a different country. It's not an issue with social networks. You can send the invites, gather the responses, update the venue and correspond with everyone through a single page to make sure everything goes smoothly.

Travel

Brochures are designed to make every destination look wonderful, which is where reviews sites like TripAdvisor (www.tripadvisor.com) can help with a dose of realism. Like all such sites there is a danger that the reviews are not entirely impartial – either too flattering or hypercritical because of some bias on the part of the writer. However, you'll get a general consensus and if the same problems are consistently mentioned, then it should act as a warning signal.

Above: Although they can offer helpful advice on an unfamiliar destination, remember that opinions aired on such sites as TripAdvisor are purely personal.

ORGANIZE YOUR WORKING LIFE

Business is just as social as your personal life. There are many social media tools designed to help you in your career – whether it's finding a new job, developing your skills or promoting your business.

Hot Tip

As well as the destinations, comments by TripAdvisor users are also rated for their helpfulness. Click 'Check this score', which is beside the review, to see how much weight to give to their opinions.

Promote Yourself

You can go a long way to create 'Brand You' by adding your profile and developing a rich network of connections on LinkedIn. You'll be in good company, as it includes many of the world's top business people. US President Barack Obama has his own profile, as does the British Prime Minister and most politicians in the UK. While LinkedIn is the major business network, there may be other more specialist social media sites linked to your particular industry, such as Model Mayhem (www.modelmayhem.com) for professional models and photographers.

Promote Your Career

As well as building your brand, most business social networks also act as recruitment centres. Sites like LinkedIn will suggest jobs you may be interested in, based on your profile, as well as providing recruitment managers with the search tools to head hunt people who match their requirements. In addition, there are recruitment sites, such as Monster (www.monster.com) that have applications like BeKnown that enable them to post jobs directly to social networks, such as Facebook or Twitter.

Above: Use social media to give your career prospects a boost by searching quickly for suitable vacancies.

Promote Your Business

As well as personal branding many social media sites enable businesses to build their profile and promote their brands. This can include status updates on everything from new product releases to new starters and much in between. Social games can also provide an element of fun, while promoting the brand, and link in with more traditional press and TV advertising campaigns. For a more direct conversation with customers many businesses also run their own blogs.

Connect With Other Businesses

While businesses are often in competition with each other, the individuals within those organisations face many of the same issues. Although they could talk about these with colleagues, social media sites provide them with a global forum in which to share experiences. Sites like LinkedIn offer industry groups, for anything from automotive engineering to retail, where people can exchange views on current issues. Many professional and trade bodies also run their own communities and groups to bring like-minded professionals together.

FAD OR NOT? WHAT'S THE EVIDENCE?

Wherever you look the statistics are different. The one thing they have in common is that they are huge. Social media is not going to go away soon, so shouldn't you join in?

So Many Social Media Users

Facebook has reached one billion active users a month worldwide, according to Google AdPlanner. They will share more than 3.5 billion pieces of content – that is web links, news stories, blog posts and such – a week. The picture for the individual is a little easier to take in: he or she will have an average of 130 friends and spend the majority of the time talking with about 20 per cent of them. Twitter has more than 100 million active users – that is people who log in at least once a month – while LinkedIn has much the same. There are estimated to be more than 181 million blogs around the world (up from 36 million five years ago). More than 72 hours of video are uploaded to YouTube every minute.

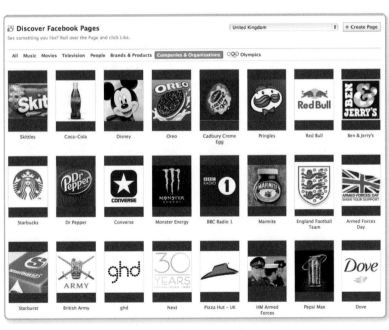

Above: Most major companies have an online presence, allowing them to reach more consumers than ever before.

SOCIAL MEDIA IN TRADITIONAL MEDIA

The traditional broadcast model has turned from a one-way conversation – from one to many – into a two-way social dialogue, where many talk to many. Both broadcast and print media now openly source many of their stories from Twitter – from breaking news to celebrity feuds – and will often include comments and information taken from social media sites within stories. Through their online sites, most media publishers solicit comments and likes as well as encourage sharing of content on social media sites. Some, like the *Guardian* in the UK encourage people to go online and write blog entries to be published in their Comment section. Also, how many article bylines have you seen recently that don't also list the author's Twitter or Facebook username?

Above: It is now the norm for readers to comment on and share stories that affect them.

SOCIAL MEDIA IN ADVERTISING

Once, the product or brand was always the focus of advertising. But that is changing, particularly online. With the popularity of social media, advertisers like Coca Cola and Volkswagen are using online and even TV ads to promote events on Facebook, Twitter or YouTube, rather than pitch the product directly. So, for example, companies like Ritz have used ads to point people to online competitions they're running on Facebook.

SOCIAL MEDIA IN GOVERNMENT

Whether in or out of power, most politicians now recognize the potency of social media to reach their constituents quickly and directly. There can be downsides, however, such as when a message or picture that should be confidential is accidentally published,

Hot Tip

Tweets have a very short lifespan. If you see one that you want to keep and refer back to, save it as a Favorite. To do so, hover your mouse over the tweet and click the Favorite link.

as one US congressman who tweeted a photo of his private parts found out. But generally, it is a powerful way of both disseminating information and gathering ideas. US Space Agency NASA uses Twitter to send out information about its programmes as well as photos. When Canada wanted to get the public involved in a discussion on what the government's approach to social innovation should be, they used a 'crowdsourced wiki' – that is a wiki where anyone could add articles or edit existing ones in a combined effort to determine official policy. Similarly, in the UK, anyone can create an e-petition and, by sharing it on social media, attempt to get the 100,000 signatures needed to be considered for debate in Parliament. More mundanely, in San Francisco you can report a pothole or faulty streetlight to the council direct from your Facebook account. These are early steps in what will be an increasingly pervasive use of social media.

Above: It is more than a way to organize your social life – governments and their agencies are now harnessing the power of social media.

TYPES OF SOCIAL MEDIA

There is such a variety to social media, with new applications emerging all the time, that it is hard to categorise them. There is also a great deal of overlap. For example, most social networks allow you to share photos and videos, which is the main focus of media-sharing sites like Flickr and YouTube. Roughly there are 10 main types of social media.

SOCIAL NETWORKS

These are the most familiar type of social media, thanks to the great popularity of Facebook and LinkedIn. Social networks let you connect with people who have a common background and shared interests.

MICROBLOGGING/LIFESTREAMING

This is virtually synonymous with Twitter, which is by far the biggest microblogging site. Very short (micro) blog posts – less than 140 characters on Twitter – are pushed out to anyone who has subscribed to your updates. You can read the updates of those in your network, as well as discovering new people to follow.

BLOGGING

A blog allows you to publish content online – whether it's your daily diary or your thoughts on German philosophers. Ultimately, you want your blog to be read. The best way to achieve this is to encourage feedback and debate by allowing comments. Online forums also enable members to debate questions. Whatever your interests, you should find many blogs or forums that suit you among the hundreds of millions available online.

SOCIAL BOOKMARKING

Sites like Delicious (delicious.com) and Faves (faves.com) allow you to save and manage bookmarks – or links – to web pages and other resources you come across on the Internet. As it's easy to amass hundreds of bookmarks, you can also tag them with keywords that make them easier to search and share, if you choose, with others. When you view someone else's bookmarks there's usually a description and sometimes an opinion about the site, which can help you decide if you want to visit.

SOCIAL NEWS

These services post news stories and blog posts, or links to them, for you to vote on. The most popular, that is those that get the most votes, are displayed more prominently and for longer. Among the main social news sites are Digg (digg.com) and Reddit (www.reddit.com).

MEDIA SHARING

Upload your photos or videos and share them with just family and friends or open them to public viewing, as you prefer. Among the most popular sites are YouTube and Flickr. These sites also allow you to add a profile and invite comments on your photos and videos.

LOCATION-BASED NETWORKING SERVICES

You may also hear these services referred to as geosocial networks. They mix information, or mashup as the technically-minded put it, about

Above: Out and about? No problem: sites like Yelp help you find what you need whilst on the move.

Hot Tip

If you've just moved into an area, download a location-sharing app onto your mobile and you'll get the lowdown on your new neighbourhood as you walk around.

Above: The internet is bursting with sites for every possible interest, even for the cat men and women among us.

where you are with recommendations for places you can go locally, such as restaurants, hotels, places of interest and so on. Popular applications include Foursquare (foursquare.com) and Yelp (www.yelp.co.uk).

SPECIAL-INTEREST SOCIAL NETWORKS

If you have a particular passion – such as music or travel – you can probably find a niche social networking site that is targeted to your interests. The range is wide, covering everything from pets (www.catster.com, www.dogster.com) and music sharing (www.last.fm, www.spotify.com) to social review sites like TripAdvisor for travel and Epinions (www.epinions.com) for virtually everything else. Several now link in with other social networks, like Facebook, so they can show you what your friends recommend.

Social Virtual Gaming

These are types of online games that can be played in virtual worlds, such as World of Warcraft, or through a social network, like Farmville, which tens of millions of people play through Facebook.

Social Virtual Worlds

These are picturesque worlds, which you inhabit in 'real time' with other users. Your character is represented by an avatar that interacts with the others. Second Life is the most famous.

SETTING UP YOUR ACCOUNT

Most social media sites follow similar processes when it comes to setting up a new account. This will typically involve creating a profile, so you need to consider how much personal information to share.

GETTING STARTED

Most social media sites offer a tour of the features they offer, or let you explore the site without becoming a member so you can be sure that it's right for you. However, there'll come a point when you will need to register. While each individual site has its own specific requirements, most will include:

→ **Email address**: This will be used by the site to communicate with you, such as notifying you when someone has commented on what you've written, and to pass on messages from other users.

→ **Username**: This has, for obvious reasons, to be unique. If your first choice is not available the site will usually suggest various options, based on it. Be careful to make this something you are comfortable with, as it will become part of your online identity. For example, 2fluffybunnyears might seem quite beguiling for a moment, and could be fine on Facebook, but is unlikely to give the right impression on career-minded LinkedIn users.

Above: When choosing a username, link it to the type of site you're joining. Cheesy or silly names don't look good on a professional network.

⮕ **Password**: This is usually between six and eight characters; often requiring a combination of letters and at least one number.

⮕ **Date of birth**: Often used as part of the mechanism to return more relevant suggestions for friends or people you may know. Some sites use it publicly, though if you're self-conscious about your age you can choose to leave off your birth year, or not publish it at all.

⮕ **Security question**: This is to check that it is a person and not a spam robot that's trying to join. You need to fill in the letters and numbers in the image – called a CAPTCHA (Completely Automated Public Turing test to tell Computers and Humans Apart). If, as is often the case, you can't make out what they are you can either refresh the screen to get a new image or have the characters spoken to you.

⮕ **Activation email**: Once successfully registered, you'll usually be sent an email to the address you entered. You'll need to click on the link in the email to activate your account and show you have a working email address.

Above: Entering the numbers and letters from the security question displayed on the site is a vital part of registering your new account.

SETTING UP YOUR PROFILE

This is possibly the most important part of joining any social media site, as it will fundamentally shape how useful it is to you. Recommendations for friends and people who share your interests will largely depend on your profile.

Personal Information to Include

The information you put here will be shared with other people on the site. In most cases, the same information or a shortened version of it, will appear in search results on Google or Bing etc. Generally, you will be asked to fill in details of where you live, where you were educated, what you're doing, what your likes are and so on.

> # Hot Tip
> When filling in your profile you can decide who this information is shared with, through the privacy settings. If you are at all worried, leave personal details out, as you can always add them later.

Real or Fake Name

On some sites identity is everything. You won't get to many reunions if you don't use your real name on Friends Reunited. For other sites, like Twitter or YouTube, anonymity may not seem an issue, at first. However, as you build your circle of friends and followers, it gives them more confidence if they feel they are talking to a real person and not someone using a fake persona.

Lurking

Not everyone who uses social media gets actively involved in all aspects. Roughly 40 per cent of Twitter users don't tweet, they simply log in to their timelines to see what other people are saying. Lurking, that is browsing a site without ever posting anything, is fine. It's a good way to get to know a site initially and see whether you want to get involved. Ultimately though, you'll get more from social media by taking part.

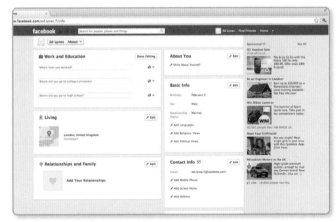

Above: It is up to you how much information you reveal about yourself on Facebook: remember that everything you include will be shared with others.

SAFETY AND PRIVACY

Much is made of the dangers of social media sites, but like everything else online, if you take a few sensible precautions it is extremely unlikely that you will experience any problems.

STAYING SAFE

The same rules apply to meeting people online as in the real world. Be very cautious about giving out any personal details – especially your phone number, address, full birth date or place of birth, as these can be useful for identity thieves. Certainly don't publish these in your profile.

If you're using location-aware social networks, be particularly careful about saying where you live as people will know when you're not there. Equally, you shouldn't publicize family holiday dates, as this could reveal to burglars when you are away and your home is empty.

SECURITY OPTIONS

Most sites have a series of security options that control who can see your personal information and view your photos or videos. However, they are not always obvious. Make a point when you join a site of finding where they are and setting them to the most secure level. You can always relax them later when you know more about how the site works.

Above: Choose the level of privacy to apply to your account, according to how much you wish to reveal to the wider world.

USING SOCIAL MEDIA AT WORK

Because they are so much a part of the fabric of our daily lives, many companies are relaxed about staff accessing social media from their work computers. After all, it may be that you are accessing a company account. It's likely that your employer will track what you are doing and how much time you spend doing it. So it's important, when you've finished, to always log out of any social networking site on a computer where other people have access. Similarly, don't select the option to stay logged in when accessing sites on a public computer.

PRIVACY

In the attempt to offer more personalized services, social media sites have sometimes tried to introduce policies that many users have felt invaded their privacy. Keep an eye on privacy settings to make sure that by default you're not being asked to share more than you're comfortable with.

Above: If you use a shared computer, ensure the Remember me box remains unchecked otherwise the next user will be able to access your account.

KEEPING INFORMATION AND PHOTOS SAFE

When you publish content on your self-hosted blog, you control it. You can delete it, change it, or remove part of it, for example, a photo or caption. With other social media you don't always have the same rights. If you post a photo on a site like Facebook that you later remove, any copies that your friends have made will still

Hot Tip

Even if you are only planning to connect with friends and family on the social networks you join, you should still regard any information you give as being publicly available and act accordingly.

exist and be displayed. That's why it's important to ensure you set the privacy settings for every site you join, at the beginning.

For example, Facebook lets you set the default privacy level for your status updates and photos. It also has a range of other privacy options, which cover how you connect with people and how content is handled, that also lets you change who can view past posts.

THIRD-PARTY ACCESS

Social media sites often work together to deliver more personalized services. For example, several companies have partnered with Facebook so that when you arrive at their website you immediately hear the music you like (Pandora, www.pandora.com) or see relevant reviews by your friends at Yelp or TripAdvisor.

They can only access information you have agreed to make public, but you do have the option to turn this feature off, if you prefer. Typically, you will have to authorize an application that tries to use information from any of your social media accounts – such as iPhoto wanting to upload photos direct to Facebook or Tweetdeck for viewing Twitter on a smartphone. Permission can be revoked at any time.

Left: You can use apps that are able to access your Twitter account, such as from your smartphone or tablet. You can withdraw permission, at any time, from within Twitter.

TRACKING YOUR MOVEMENTS

Your personal information is worth money. There are many companies willing to spend significant amounts to get to know more about your browsing habits, interests and lifestyle choices. They do so largely through cookies, small files sent to your PC, smartphone or tablet, which store information that can be accessed if you revisit the site.

How these cookies are used will depend on the site. Some sites use it to track what you've got in your shopping cart to make it easier to buy online on this and future visits. Many say it's to personalize your experience on their site, so they can make offers and suggestions for new friends or products that are more relevant to you.

There is a new EU cookie law, which all member states are supposed to introduce; however, few have done so. This law makes it compulsory for sites to give users more information about cookies, so that they can consent to them being used. Some social network sites are sending data about you – without you knowing – to other companies. You can stop this.

Above: Cookies are used by organisations and retailers to personalize your internet experience, but beware: they sometimes pass on data without your knowledge.

> ## Hot Tip
> There are several programs that you can 'add-in' to your browser, which will show and block any tracking activity. Among them are Adblock Plus (www.adblockplus.org) and Ghostery (www.ghostery.com).

COPYRIGHT

Once something has been published to a social networking site – particularly photos – it can be difficult to remove them. You should check that you have the right to publish them before you do so and be careful about who you share them with.

SOCIAL NETWORKS

Once you post a comment or a photo on a social network, you effectively lose control over what happens to that content. It is easily copied and passed on. On Facebook, for example, the terms of agreement mean that you grant them a free licence to use any content you post. In effect, it means that they can hold the content you upload and show it on a Facebook page to the people you allow to access it. These people can also copy the content – such as photos – and use it on their pages. Should you decide later to remove a photo, you have no rights to insist that anyone who has copied it, does the same.

Above: Sites, such as YouTube, ensure that users have full access to their copyright rules.

> # Hot Tip
> Unless you're a lawyer, the terms of use and copyright can be very difficult to read. For a cut-down version in plain English check out the FAQs available on most sites.

Check the Small Print

For this reason, you should be careful how widely you share your content. This is controlled by the privacy settings. Each site has its own copyright rules, so if you are concerned, you should check these before you start using the site fully.

CONTENT AND COPYRIGHT

Generally content falls into four main groups:

- **Public domain**: Free for you to do what you want with it, whether that is to use it as is, change it or even sell it.

- **Copyleft/free-use content/Creative Commons License system**: Where content is generally available to use but some rights are reserved. This can cover a range of activities from simply personal use to anything short of selling it on.

- **Copyright**: The traditional standard where the owner reserves all rights. Except for fair-use you need the owner's express permission to use the content in any way.

- **Fair-use**: Legally allows you to use a small section of copyrighted material, such as a quote, comment or sentence from a news story. You would normally need to cite the source, but do not have to get written permission to use it.

PHOTO SHARING

Unless you took the photograph yourself, it's likely that the copyright of any picture you come across, whether it's from a Google images search or downloaded from another site, belongs to someone else. Before you use the image, you should contact the photographer to ask permission. If they are happy for you to use the photograph, it is normal etiquette to include a link back to the original source or at least give a credit to the photographer.

Above: Always ensure that you are not infringing anyone's copyright by seeking the photographer's permission before you share a photo.

PHOTOS ON BLOGS

A good source for photos to use on your blog is a photo-sharing library such as Flickr. Usefully, they have very clear guidelines about copyright. You can set the licence for your own photos and content in Owner settings. The licensing system is based on the Creative Commons License, which is used on many sites around the web. It allows you to say whether individual photos are available to use, what attribution is needed, and if they can be used in commercial work or just for personal use.

QUOTING OTHERS

You need to be similarly careful about quoting text, whether it's a news item, blog post or comment. Some authors wanting to drive traffic to their website are happy if you copy an entire blog post – provided you link to them – while others fiercely protect their copyright. Many bloggers will mark their posts using the Creative Commons License system so you know how you can use their content.

Above: If you're setting up your own blog, there are thousands of templates to choose from, but the best ones usually come with a price tag.

BLOG TEMPLATES

There are many freely available templates for use on your blog, whether you are using a hosted site or self-hosting one. There are also premium templates available for a fee, which can be quite substantial. Typically, these include more advanced features and widgets. You need to check what is included with the template. The great photo that attracted you to buy it may not be part of the package if the designer hasn't got copyright. There may also be restrictions about modifying the template, selling it on or using it on more than one site.

WHAT YOU NEED TO GET STARTED

You have all the tools you need for social media on your computer, smartphone or tablet.

SOCIAL MEDIA TOOLS FOR HOME AND WORK

As social media sites are online they are freely accessed from any computer you use, whether at home or work. That is part of their popularity (with the result that you may find your employer blocks staff access to Facebook or Twitter during office hours so there are no distractions from work).

Easy Access

Traditionally, sites have been viewed through the browser – Internet Explorer, Firefox, Chrome or Safari – and that's still the main way to connect. However, as social media has become such a big part of our lives, direct access is now being built-in to computers. Apple's new operating system Mountain Lion is integrated with Twitter, so you can sign in and manage your account from your Mac, without using the browser, as well as tweet links and photos from a range of other programs.

SOCIAL MEDIA TOOLS ON THE GO

While you can access social media through the browser on your smartphone or tablet, it often isn't the best experience. Both Twitter and Facebook have special mobile apps that give full access to all the features of the site. There are also dozens of third-party programs, such as Tweetbot or Twitterdeck for Twitter, and MyPad or Friendly for Facebook, that offer additional features.

MANAGING MULTIPLE ACCOUNTS

Once you get hooked on social media, it's quite likely that you'll have a number of different accounts, from Flickr to Facebook, Twitter to YouTube, Pinterest and more. While they all have apps to manage them, it would be simpler to have them all accessible in one place. There are various online sites where you can manage and post your updates in one place:

➔ **Seesmic Ping (seesmic.com):** This is a free hub where you can link up to 30 major social networks.

➔ **HootSuite (hootsuite.com):** Available online and as a desktop or mobile app, this lets you update Twitter, Facebook, LinkedIn and WordPress together, as well as schedule when posts are sent.

➔ **Bliss Control (blisscontrol.com):** Doesn't access your posts but shows you how to change 12 different settings, such as your profile picture, on 13 social media sites.

Above: Mobile apps for sites such as Twitter ensure that you don't miss a tweet! (pictured: iPhone app for Twitter).

Above: HootSuite allows you to manage multiple social profiles in one place.

Hot Tip

You never know when inspiration will strike, so you should make sure you have a notebook application on your mobile to write down your ideas for your blog, add a photo or even a sketch. Better still, most sites have a mobile app that lets you update your blog on the move.

NETIQUETTE

Like every community, the net has its own etiquette, or rules of engagement, which is referred to as netiquette.

RULES OF SOCIAL MEDIA

Forums in particular will often post the rules for any members wanting to join in the conversation. Generally, the way you treat people online is no different to the normal rules of polite behavior in everyday life.

YOUR PROFILE INFORMATION

It should be about the real you, unless there's a good reason. It is social media, after all, so it is not very social if one party is not sharing any information or is hiding behind a different identity. There are some exceptions. People in certain jobs – the police, teachers and so on – are advised to be discreet about their true identity.

PROFILE PICTURE

It is best to be you, rather than a logo or avatar. Use a photo you're comfortable with. If that is from a decade or so ago, fine, but remember that this may become evident as recent photos of you are tagged and shown in your timeline or Twitter feed.

State Your Cause

If you want company in the photo frame, Twibbon (twibbon.com) will let you represent a campaign with

Hot Tip

Photos should ideally be a face or head and shoulders shot, rather than one of you in the background, and reasonably good quality (that is, not blurred or with red eyes).

Above: Twibbon is your virtual protest placard: stand up for your cause from the comfort of your own home.

your profile image (or start your own), ranging from homeless animals to End Child Marriage.

FRIENDING

It is not compulsory to accept friend requests or follow people who ask. You really don't have to say yes, unless it's your mother.

Unfriending

If you do decide later to unfriend or unfollow someone you can do it quietly. They will probably not know, unless they use a browser plugin like Unfriend Finder for Facebook or subscribe to sites like Who.Unfollowed.Me (who.unfollowed.me) for Twitter.

FOLLOWING CELEBRITIES

Part of the attraction of social media is following celebrities who also have accounts. Just don't be surprised if you can't get Lady Gaga or Lord Sugar to follow you back.

COMMUNICATING

Commenting on other people's blogs or walls is a good way of interacting and will lead them to respond in kind. There is, of course, an etiquette to consider:

Above: Sites like this enable you to keep track of your friends (or ex-friends, perhaps?).

➔ Make your comment about the point that is being made, not what you think about the mental status of the person who made it.

→ If you do get into an angry and aggressive exchange with another user, it is called flaming and on forums, in particular, it will lead to you being banned.

→ Racist remarks, comments likely to offend religious groups and pornographic posts are also unacceptable.

→ Don't write in CAPITAL LETTERS. This is the online equivalent of SHOUTING!

→ When you make a comment, make sure it is on topic. If you change the topic, such as on a forum, make sure there isn't already a thread on the subject.

LINKING TO OTHER PEOPLE

If your blog post is a reaction to a news story or what someone else has written on their blog, link to it. If you are using a story this way, add a comment or thought that shows why it interested you. Where you are linking to someone else's content make sure you have the right to do so, and follow any conditions they set.

Give to Receive

If you like someone's blog, tell them. You'd want to know if it was the other way round wouldn't you? Virtually every blog now has a button to press if you want to Like/Share/Tweet a post.

Hot Tip

If something's worth saying once, say it four or five times. If you've got news, post it, suitably adapted, on Facebook, Twitter, your blog, your Flickr page and YouTube channel (if relevant).

PROMOTING YOURSELF OR YOUR BUSINESS

The rule is don't advertise, unless it is specifically allowed. Some people get round this by adding a promo or mini ad with their name, when they sign off on a comment. For example, A. N. Author: Read my new ebook *Adventures in Casablanca* out now.

Above: Most wesbites have a Twitter button like this that lets you tweet the link to your followers.

LOBBYING

Some communities – or individuals – are using social media to lobby for their cause. They put a lot of effort in and will be quite forceful in asking for money as well as support. If you're planning such a site, here are some points worth bearing in mind:

→ It is a social conversation. Promote your cause as if you were at a networking event or party, rather than pushing the message as you would in a full-blooded awareness campaign.

→ Your cause may not be their cause, and pestering won't convert them.

→ Urging people to 'Like' your page on Facebook works – you get to know the profile of the people supporting you and can message them directly.

Above: The softly softly approach works just as well in the virtual world as it does in the real: resist the urge to be in-your-face, however passionate your beliefs.

→ Even so, it is usually better to push your message on your wall rather than sending a direct message to individuals, who may find it annoying and intrusive.

RULE OF THIRDS

As a rough guide when using social media for marketing, think of the rule of thirds:

→ Promote your own business and ideas in your updates for a third of the time.

➔ Push content from other sources about the topics that interest you a third of the time.

➔ Communicate with people directly for a third of the time.

DISCLOSE YOUR LINKS

It is important to disclose any commercial links you have with a product or person you are discussing. If you are writing about a client in your blog or in a tweet. you should add the fact. If you are using an affiliate link (where you are paid a percentage of any purchase that follows from the customer following the link on your site, such as Amazon) you should make this clear (in your post, in a tweet or on your blog site). If you are generous in promoting others, even where you have no direct commercial link, it is more likely that they will promote you later, when needed.

HOW OFTEN TO POST OR TWEET?

Ultimately, this depends on the time you have available. The life of a tweet is around 40 minutes at most, so you can happily post the same tweet several times a day.

However, people do unfollow noisy tweeters (those who tweet too often) particularly if there's nothing original in what they say. Because Facebook is a longer read, and is more suited to posting photos or video clips, you can usefully update several times a day. Blogs take much more work. If you're only updating monthly, readers are likely to drift off as you're not building any momentum. Weekly is workable, but two or three times a week would give you a chance to develop your following.

Hot Tip

Write your blog when the muse comes and schedule your posts to publish later. That way you have material ready to cover the times when you're too busy, or not in the frame of mind to blog.

Above: Plug-ins like let you schedule the publication date for your blog posts, in advance.

SOCIAL NETWORKS

NETWORKS WITH A PURPOSE

Social networks give you the tools to take your social circle online, and communicate freely with all types of people who share your interests.

WHAT IS A SOCIAL NETWORK?

A social network is an online community, such as Facebook or LinkedIn, that allows you to communicate and share messages, pictures, videos and thoughts with other people who have similar interests. You can access these social networks through your computer (PC or Mac), tablet (iPad or Nexus) or mobile (iPhone, Blackberry or Android or Windows smartphone)

Above: LinkedIn is one of the most popular business social networks; here it is viewed on an iPad.

WHO USES SOCIAL NETWORKS?

Social networks are like an online village. They contain people you know well, like friends and family, business colleagues, people you've just met through friends, a community of people with a common interest including complete strangers you somehow got talking to. This community is not restricted to one location, so you can connect with someone across the world as easily as the person in the next street. At the end of the day, they are also there for socializing – a virtual gossip fest between old friends and new on everything that's happening.

TYPES OF SOCIAL NETWORK

Just as in any community, social networks are constantly evolving, with new ones opening all the time. While some of the bigger sites, like Facebook, remain universally popular others have had to reinvent themselves. MySpace, once bigger than Facebook, has gone from the leading blog and social network to a music-based 'social entertainment' centre. While there is some overlap, most social networks will fit into one of three broad categories.

General Interest

These all-purpose networks will help you connect with friends you already know as well as make new ones.

Facebook – www.facebook.com – The best-known and most popular site, founded in 2004, with nearly a billion active users. A free service, most of the members (81 per cent) come from outside the US and Canada. As well as the easy contact it provides families and friends, it is used by celebrities, political figures, lobbying groups, charities and many companies.

Bebo – www.bebo.com – Like Facebook it has a timeline for you to share what's going on in your life. You can share photos, videos, stories and special events. The Lifestream Platform will show not only your Bebo updates but also all your friends' posts from Facebook, MySpace, YouTube, Flickr, Twitter and Delicious.

Above: Like many social networks, Bebo allows you to share what is going on in your life with your friends.

Orkut – www.orkut.com – One of Google's social networks, you can sign up using your Gmail account. It is particularly strong in Brazil, India and the US. It has all the features you'd expect for finding friends, sending messages, uploading photos and videos and blogging.

Tagged/Hi5 – www.tagged.com/www.hi5.com – These are the sites for meeting new people. While the focus of traditional social networking sites has been on maintaining existing connections, these new social discovery sites are about discovering new relationships. Tagged, along with it subsidiary Hi5, claims to have the largest social discovery network in the world with 330 million members in 220 countries. They use special search, social games and shared interests to help like-minded people meet.

Badoo – badoo.com – Another site making the evolution to a social network site for meeting new people, locally and globally.

Specialist Interest

These social networks have a special focus or theme, whether it's a shared interest like music, films or cars, or a common background such as school, university or workplace.

Myspace – www.myspace.com – This has changed from general-interest social network to a social entertainment destination. In effect, it connects you with people who have a mutual interest in music, celebrities, TV, film and games.

Above: Music aficionados and fashionistas head to Buzznet to discover the latest news and gossip.

Buzznet – www.buzznet.com – Describes itself as the web's largest social magazine. With a strong youth bias it is a community for self-confessed pop culture addicts, music lovers and trendsetters. Members are rewarded for sharing videos, photos or news by being buzzed. The top content contributors – or buzzmakers – are shown across the site.

Friends Reunited – www.friendsreunited.com – This was the British social networking pioneer. It started by reuniting old school friends, then expanded to cover university and workplaces. Now it acts as a sort of collective national memory bank, celebrating 'every blast from the past'.

Business Interest

While sites like Facebook have an area for companies – Facebook Pages – that is not their primary purpose. There are social networks with a focus on business. These professional networks enable you to meet people who can help you in your career as well as communicate with others in the same industry about common topics of interest.

LinkedIn – www.linkedin.com – Launched in 2003, this is the biggest and best known of the professional networks on the Internet, with more than 160 million members in over 200 countries. It is all about making contacts. Your personal profile includes your career history and recommendations from previous colleagues and employers, which can be seen by your network of connections.

Hot Tip

On LinkedIn you can expand your network by asking the contacts of existing contacts to join.

Xing – www.xing.com – This is a social network with more than 12 million members, largely in Europe. It provides a platform for not only finding useful business contacts but also a new job or work assignment. There are more than 50,000 specialist groups for members as well as real-world events that can be arranged and managed online.

Ryze – www.ryze.com – Difficult to guess, but the name Ryze is designed to reflect how professional networking helps people 'rise up'. A smaller network, but globally spread, with around 500,000 members in 200 countries, who benefit from a free networking-oriented homepage and easy messaging.

LINKING SOCIAL NETWORKS

Just as we are connected to a web of social networking sites, so the sites themselves can connect to each other. It means that when you update one account, say LinkedIn, the very same information can be posted to your Facebook status. For this to happen you have to give your permission – and so does the network. Previously, you could post your tweets from Twitter to LinkedIn, but now Twitter has stopped that (although the reverse, where LinkedIn users can share their status updates on Twitter is still possible).

FACEBOOK

From its origins as a college-based site, Facebook has become the most popular social networking site on the Internet with nearly one billion active users a month.

STEP BY STEP: SET UP YOUR ACCOUNT

Facebook is all about connecting with families and friends. You can share photos, music, links and videos, play games, follow celebrities or companies, enter competitions and sign up for, or organize, events. The following step-by-step guide explains how to get started, but please note that as the Facebook site is constantly refreshed the actual steps may vary.

1. Use your browser to go to the Facebook home page and you'll see the Sign Up box. Note the promise that: 'It's free and always will be.'

2. Type in your details – first name, last name and email address. Repeat your email address as a check that you typed it correctly the first time. It's important that it's correct, as this is where the email to confirm and activate your membership is sent.

3. Enter a password. The most secure passwords contain both numbers and letters.

4. Select your gender by clicking the appropriate option.

Left: Enter your details as requested to start the registration process on Facebook.

5. Enter your birthday using the arrows beside Day, Month and Year to select the correct options. Don't worry, this doesn't have to appear in your profile. It is a security measure to make sure you're above the minimum age of 13. It also ensures that younger people only have access to age-appropriate content.

Above: Picture 1: search your email accounts.

6. By clicking the Sign Up button you are agreeing to the Terms and Conditions for using the site. If you want to see what you are signing up to, which very few do, click on the Terms of Use or Privacy Policy link.

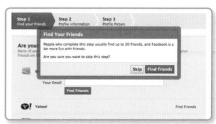

Above: Picture 2: agree to Find Friends.

7. As soon as you are registered, Facebook tries to connect you with people. The first step is to search through your email contacts list and see if any match existing Facebook members (*see* Pictures 1 and 2). Step 2 is to fill in some basic information about you, while Step 3 is to add a picture to your profile. You can carry out these steps using the on-screen instructions or click Skip This Step to come back to it later.

Above: Picture 3: click on the link to confirm your details.

8. Once complete, you come to your own Welcome page. You'll see a message at the top prompting you to confirm your email address (*see* Picture 3). This is the final stage of the sign-up process. Go to your email account, open the message from Facebook and click on the link to activate your account (*see* Picture 4).

Above: Picture 4: you are finished. Now you can add posts, photos and more.

STEP BY STEP: FILL IN YOUR PROFILE

Once you are a member you need to add your details. People want to be sure that the Cathy Jones they are contacting is the one they went to school with and not a complete stranger. Typically, a profile is just a collection of facts about you, such as where you go to school or work, what interests you have, your favourite music, TV shows or quotations and so on.

Hot Tip

If it's not a personal account you want, but one for a band, business, product, cause or community, you should set up a Facebook Page instead. Click the Create a Page link beneath the Sign Up box.

1. You can access your profile anytime by clicking your name in the blue navigation bar at the top of the page.

2. Click the +Add Profile Picture to add a photo, then Upload Photo and choose the image you want (see Pictures 1–3).

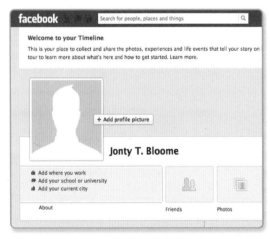

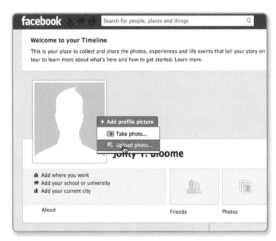

Above: Picture 1: add a profile picture

Above: Picture 2: upload your chosen image.

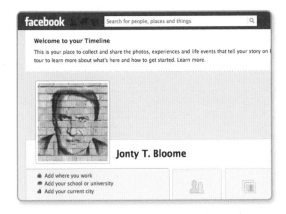

facebook   Search for people, places and things   🔍

Welcome to your Timeline
This is your place to collect and share the photos, experiences and life events that tell your story on
tour to learn more about what's here and how to get started. Learn more.

Jonty T. Bloome

🔒 Add where you work
🎓 Add your school or university
📍 Add your current city

Hot Tip

Your profile page is now based on a timeline format, which lists in date order your important events, such as a graduation or anniversary. It also shows your regular posts, such as status updates.

Left: Picture 3: all done, profile photo added.

3. Add more information by clicking the About link under the photo area or the Update Info button on the right-hand side.

4. The information you add is grouped into several categories. To change your details simply click the Edit button.

5. Work and education is for details of where you went to school, college or university and where you have worked.

6. Once you have completed the information for a particular field, click the downward-pointing arrow beside the globe.

7. This drop-down list lets you select who can see this information on your profile. By default it's Public. That means anyone on Facebook can see it and it will also show in search engine results.

8. You can change this privacy setting so that only you see this information, or Friends. Select Custom and you can be even more specific so that only selected people or groups of people – like close family – can view it. Alternatively, you can block named people from seeing it.

9. Back in your profile continue to add more information:

    - **Living**: Where you are, as well as where you consider your hometown to be.

    - **Relationships and Family**: The people close to you. You can include a photo as well as specify their relationship to you.

Above: Find your hometown and current location from the drop-down menu.

- **About You**: This is your space to share what you think people would like to know.

- **Basic Info**: Your age, sex, etc. and some more profound issues like your religious or political beliefs. Remember the description box is small for a reason. This isn't the place to promote your faith or cause.

- **Contact Info**: For details of how you can be contacted, via Facebook or offsite through your mobile, website etc.

- **Favorite Quotations**: Where you can include the sayings that inspire or amuse you.

10. It's worth reminding yourself to click the Save button every time you make a change otherwise it will be lost.

Above: By checking the Public option, all Facebook users will be able to see this information.

FINDING FRIENDS & FAMILY

A social network isn't social without friends. There are various ways to find them.

Search

Available at the top of every page. As soon as you start typing, Facebook tries to guess possible matches and displays a list. If there are none you recognize, click See more results ... In the results are clues to identify if it's the right person, such as where they work or studied, and if they have any mutual friends. Click on their name to see their profile page or the link to send a message.

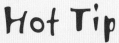

Hot Tip

Facebook tags are labels that identify people in an update, photo or video. When you tag someone, , Facebook notifies them. The posted item can be seen in their timeline as well as yours.

Above: The See more results option will bring up more potential contacts matching your request.

If you're sure it's the right person, befriend them by clicking the +1 Add Friend button. Your friend will have to confirm your request before they are added to your list.

Find Friends Link

Access this page through the left-hand column of your home page or the top navigation bar. There may already be a list of suggestions based on any friends you added. Click on See All beside People you may know and use the advanced search options to find friends based on your hometown, where you live now, schools, university, mutual friends and so on.

Facebook Suggests

When you first join Facebook it offers to search your contacts book to find friends who already have a Facebook account. While this is a quick way to get started, you must give Facebook the password for your email account. If you are at all concerned don't do it, and use other methods to find friends.

ANSWERING FRIEND REQUESTS

From time to time, you may receive friend requests. These will show as a number beside the Find Friends link on the home page and beside the icons in the top navigation bar. Click on the link and confirm the request. If you're not sure who the person is, you can click their picture to see their profile, or the Mutual Friends link to see whom you both know. If you're still not sure whether you want to accept, click the Not Now button. This hides the request. When you're ready to deal with it, select See hidden requests.

GOODBYE FRIEND

It's likely that at some point you will want to 'unfriend' someone. You may have had a falling out, or been irritated by their posts or simply want

Above: Confirm a would-be friend's request by clicking Confirm.

to cut down your list of friends. To remove a friend, go to their profile page and click the small gear icon on the right and select Report/Block. There are three options:

- **Unsubscribe:** This is the least extreme. You unsubscribe from their posts, so you won't see their stories on your home page news feed, but they are still listed as your Facebook friend.

- **Unfriend:** They cannot post on your timeline, nor can you on theirs. There's no undo for this. If you decide to 'refriend' them you'll need to send a new friend request.

- **Block:** This is goodbye. You won't be able to see or contact each other again on Facebook.

Unfriend Finder (www.unfriendfinder.com) will let you know who has dropped you as a friend.

SUBSCRIPTIONS

Do you know Britney Spears? Or Arianna Huffington? Thought not. But you can still see their posts, even though they are not friends, among your news feed stories. Go to their home page and click the Subscribe button. You can also choose what content to view. If the Subscribe button is not visible, it means that person doesn't permit subscriptions.

You can have your own subscribers, who can view your public updates without being a friend. Go to the drop-down arrow on the top navigation bar and select Account Settings. Follow the Subscribers link and in the page that opens click the Allow Subscribers box.

Right: Subscribing to a person's page means you can view their posts.

Hot Tip

The smaller Timeline in the right-hand corner of your profile page lets you navigate over the past months and years, all the way back to birth.

USING YOUR TIMELINE

This is your profile page. The information about you is built around a Timeline – hence the name – that runs down the centre of the page. From this Timeline you can see your posts, activities and so on, at a particular time. You can go backwards and forwards in time to view what happened and add key events to the timeline, such as a wedding, graduation, etc.

Above: The large area at the top, called the Cover, can be personalized with any photo. Here, it is the same as the inset profile photo.

WHAT MAKES UP YOUR TIMELINE?

The Timeline is made up of different Facebook elements. At the top is the blue navigation bar that is standard to all pages. Underneath is a large area, called the Cover. You can personalize this with a photo that gives the page your own distinctive look. Inset is your profile photo. Key information that you gave when you set up your account, including your birthday, hometown and so on, follows. You can add any missing information you choose by clicking the relevant link. Beside your name is the Update Info button that lets you add more about you. Click the Activity Log button to see the different things you have done. The panels below link through to an associated page (if they are not all visible click the arrow on the right). These panels generally are:

- ➔ **Friends:** Thumbnail images of all your friends on Facebook.

- ➔ **Photos:** To view your albums, add others and see photos in which you are tagged.

- ➔ **Map:** Where you can track the places important to you, whether it's the location of a photo, where you live, or where something memorable happened.

- ➔ **Likes:** Lists your favourite things, shows your interests and records the pages you like.

Hot Tip

The Friends box on the Timeline includes a random mix of thumbnail images of your friends. To view the full list click See All.

Subscriptions: People you are subscribed to, who are not friends.

Events: Any events you have organized, or to which you are invited.

Notes: These may be your own, your friends' notes or drafts for a blog.

Your Timeline proper starts in the section below, with the Update Status box on the left waiting for you to post 'What's on your mind?'. On the right your friends, photos and recent activities show. These can include pages you 'Like', new subscriptions and so on. The rest of the Timeline is taken up with stories and photos grouped by date and year.

Above: You can include as little or as much information as you like on your Timeline.

YOUR ACTIVITY LOG

Should you forget what you've been up to on Facebook, the Activity Log keeps a record of all you've done, back to when you joined the site. This includes changing a photo, 'Liking' a page or commenting on someone's photo. Only you can see the log and you decide which activities to share publicly.

Manage Your Activities

The Activity Log is accessed by pressing the button on your Timeline. Click on the circle to the far right of the items for the options to control how these are shared. These include showing it prominently on your Timeline, hiding it or using the audience selector to change who can view it.

STORY-TELLING

Items in your Timeline are called Stories. These can be status updates, photos or videos, links, comments that others have added and so on. Click the star icon by a story to mark it as a favourite and it will be displayed across the whole page. It will also stay visible across your Timeline, while starred. To remove this feature, click the star icon again.

Adding a Story

To add a story you need to write in the Status Update box. This is visible near the top of most pages and will say something like 'What's on your mind?' Type your message, which can be anything from what you're doing, thinking, watching on TV to a major event in your life.

Updating the Details

You'll notice there are other buttons around the status update box. Use these to add extra elements to your post.

Above: Unclick the star icon to stop the featured story being your favourite.

- ➔ **Status**: Where you enter your message.

- ➔ **Photo**: Liven up your story by adding a photo.

- ➔ **Place**: Show on a map the location you are writing about or that features in the photograph.

- ➔ **Life event**: Appears only on the Timeline page – allows you to enter details of major changes in your world, from getting a new job to the birth of your child.

As you begin to type in the box several grey icons will appear beneath:

Tag: Who are you with? Type in a friend's name to link them with your post or photo.

Date (only on your Timeline): So you can add a year to the posting, useful if it's a photo from the past.

Location: To show where you are when posting.

Audience selector: Use the drop-down arrow to choose who you want to share this individual post with. This overrides any default you have set in the privacy settings.

- The globe shows it is publicly viewable.
- The silhouette of two heads is for friends.
- The padlock means only you can see it.
- The gear is for the custom list of people who can see it – or alternatively – are blocked from viewing it.

Above: Once you click Post, your status will be updated.

When you're happy, click the Post button for your story to be published to your Timeline and to your News Feed on your home page.

POSTING ON OTHER PEOPLE'S TIMELINES

The same Update Status box is available on your friends' pages. It has exactly the same features but this time, when you click Post, the story is published to your friends' Timeline or News Feed.

DELETING POSTS

There will be times when you want to remove a post; possibly something written on the spur of the moment you've had second thoughts about or which is no longer relevant.

➔ **On your Timeline**: Move your mouse over the post and click the Edit or Remove icon that appears. If you click Hide from Timeline then the story won't show on your Timeline, but may remain on your friends' News Feeds. It will also still show on your Activity Log, which only you can see. To get rid of it completely, select Delete...

➔ **On a friend's Timeline** – Go to your Activity Log page and find the item you posted on your friend's site. Select the circle in the right-hand column and click Delete... You can also go to their site, hover over your post and click the Edit or Delete icon.

Above: You can edit or remove a previous post by going to your Activity Log page.

MANAGING YOUR HOME PAGE

As a social network, Facebook broadcasts the news that you want to share, which can be status updates, photos, videos, links and so on. These stories are distributed via a News Feed in much the same way as the BBC, Reuters or newspapers send out their updates. Hence, the stream of stories that appears on your Home page is called your News Feed.

Hot Tip

Essentially you can delete your own posts, whether they are published on your Timeline or someone else's. You can also remove posts by other people on your Timeline but you can't delete their posts from their own Timelines.

Hot Tip

If you want to see the stories in your News Feed in the order they happened, go to the Sort menu just underneath the Status Update box and select Most Recent.

Mini-feed

The stories that appear on your profile page – or Timeline – are different. This is a mini-feed

Above: The sort option on your News Feed page allows you to order posts by Most Recent or Top Stories.

(as it used to be called) that's only about you. For example, if a friend posts a holiday snap of them holding a baby alligator, it will appear on the News Feed of your home page so you and any mutual friends can see it. It will also appear on their Timeline. Only if you add a comment, or 'Like' the photo will it appear on your Timeline.

NOTIFICATIONS

So you can know when something happens that involves you, such as a friend tagging (naming) you in a photo or someone adding a comment to your update, Facebook will send you a notification. This is normally via email or can be to your mobile. To change your notification settings:

1. Go to the drop-down arrow in the top navigation bar and select Account Settings, then Notifications in the left-hand column.

2. Select the category, such as Photos, click on the Edit icon, then choose when you want to be told about different events by ticking or unticking the relevant box.

3. Red alert notifications appear in the top-left corner of the site. The figure in the red box will show the number of new alerts you've received. Click the icon to see the notification.

4. Alert over the Friends icon: You have a new friend request.

5. Alert over the Messages icon: You have a new communication.

6. Alert over the globe icon: Shows other notifications such as comments added to your posts or invites to join in a game.

Above: To find your Notifications Settings page, go to the drop-down arrow on the right of the top navigation bar and choose Account Settings.

COMMUNICATING ON FACEBOOK

Stories – status updates – are the core of communication on Facebook. But these are just the start of the conversation.

Updates and Comments

Underneath each post you'll see a comment box with your profile picture encouraging you to write a comment. Type in your text, press return and your views are published among your friends.

Like

The famous thumbs-up icon is synonymous with Facebook. To show your appreciation of an update, comment, photo or other story click the Like link. Underneath you'll see the number of people who share your view. Click this link and a pop-up box opens to display the people who like this.

Messages

This is just like sending an email, except it's a private message to people you know on Facebook. There's no email address to remember, simply start typing their name and a list of suggestions appears.

Notes

If you have more to say than you can fit in to the Status Update box then try Notes. It has all the same options to share photos and so on. Access it through the apps in the left-hand column of the Home page.

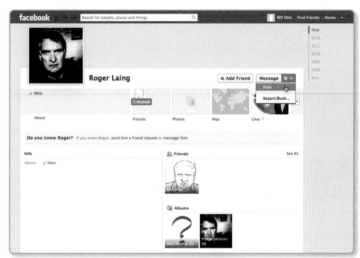

Above: Poke is the virtual equivalent of saying 'hi'.

Poke

Facebook's way to say hello, with a virtual nudge. To poke someone go to their Timeline. Click the drop-down arrow at the top and select Poke. This will appear on their home page with the option to poke you back.

Chatting

Talk in real-time with friends logged into Facebook at the same time as you. To start, show you're ready to chat. Go to the option icon at the bottom of the chat window on the right-hand side of the home page. And select Go Online to Chat.

Hot Tip

If there are certain people you don't feel like chatting with, Select Advanced Chat Settings in the options box. You can either name those you want to block or only accept invitations to chat from friends that you list.

ADDING PHOTOS

Facebook has its own photo app that makes it simple to add, change and share your photos.

Cover Photo

This is the large photo across the top of your Timeline, which you can personalize to show off your interests or an image you just like. Access your Timeline by clicking your name on the blue navigation bar, then press the Add a Cover button. A warning box reminds you the photo should be personal to your life, and is not to be used for commercial or promotional purposes.

Above: Changing your cover photo frequently adds interest to your Timeline.

Click OK, then Choose from Photos... if it is a photo that you've already got on Facebook. If not, select Upload Photo... and find the image from your computer. Once in place, you can drag or reposition the photo to fill as much of the cover area as you can, without distorting the image. Click the Save Changes button.

PROFILE PHOTO

Move your mouse over the blank placeholder where your profile picture is going and click on the Edit Profile Picture link. This gives you various options. You can choose a photo that's already on Facebook, take a photo with your webcam, that is the camera on your computer, if you have one, or upload a new feature. If the photo you choose needs adjusting, select the Edit Thumbnail option. This allows you to drag the image to resize it. Click the Scale to fit box and it will resize without distorting. Click Save when you are happy with the results.

Hot Tip

It's possible to change the photo anytime. Simply click the image there and the Change Cover menu will appear. Any photos used as Cover images are kept in the same album, Cover Photos, for easy re-use.

SHARING PHOTOS

Although it's not their primary focus, Facebook is the largest photo-sharing site on the Internet. About 200 million photos are uploaded every day. Photos are organized into their own photo albums, which can hold anything from one image to hundreds. There's no limit to how many albums you may have.

Viewing Your Photos

To view your albums, go to your timeline and click the Photos link. Underneath the albums you can browse through all the photos and

Above: In Facebook it is easy to organize your photos and videos into albums.

videos that feature you. Click on an album and re-organize or edit the photos it contains. Simply click and drag individual photos to reorder them.

Hot Tip

If you only want to see the photos your friends have posted recently, without any of the other stories, click the Photos link under Apps in the left-hand column on your Home page.

Editing Your Photos

Select Edit album and you can change individual photo details, give them a title, add a caption, tag who is in the picture, date it and more. You can also expand the album by clicking the + Add Photos button. Hover in the space beside the photo and there are further options to move the photo to another album, make it the cover picture or remove it. To delete the album completely, photos and all, press the little dustbin icon at the top of the page.

THE BIGGER PICTURE

To get a larger view of any photo, click on it and it will open in the photo viewer. At the side are options to comment and like the photo. Further actions are available if you hover your mouse over the photo until the bottom bar appears.

Above: It is possible to add information to a photo, such as a tag or a location.

- ➔ **Tag photo**: Lets you name anyone in the picture. Click on the image and a box with recent tag names opens. Alternatively, type a name in the text box at the top. When you have the right name, click the Finished tagging link.

- ➔ **Options**: Enables you to add a location or download the photo to your computer.

- ➔ **Share**: Opens a Share This Photo box with a drop-down menu that gives you the choice of putting the image on your Timeline or that of a friend, in a group or in a private message. The audience selector lets you choose who to share the photo with.

- ➔ **Like**: Give a thumbs-up to the photo.

SHARING VIDEOS

The moving image, in the shape of video, is as much a part of Facebook as the photos. You can add them to your timeline, notes and group pages. There are certain rules though.

Hot Tip

People who are not Facebook members can still view your photos. Click on your photo album and copy and paste the URL at the bottom into an email and send to your friend.

The videos must be short – less than 100 MB and no longer than 10 minutes – and not contain any copyrighted material. In particular you need to be careful of including background music tracks, or recordings of concerts. The video should be made by you or your friends and feature you or people you know.

Adding a Video

This is as simple as adding a photo and in fact uses the same app. Click the Add Photo/Video at the top of your home page, then Upload Photo/Video. Add a description, set your privacy level using the audience selector then click Choose File to select a video from your computer. When it's ready, press the Post button. Once the upload is complete, which can take a few minutes, click the Save Info button.

Playing a Video

You can play any video direct from your news feed. Simply mouse over the clip and click the Play button.

Editing a Video

Open the clip in the video viewer. Go to your Timeline, click photos, select the Your Videos page and click on the video. From here you can edit the title and description, tag the people in it, get the code to embed the video on any web page or delete it.

Recording a Video on Facebook

Instead of loading a video clip from your computer you can record one direct from your webcam. From your News Feed select Add Photo/Video then Use Webcam. Click

Above: Ensure that the video you upload includes only you or people that you know.

Hot Tip

When you click record an Adobe Flash Player Settings box may open, which requests permission to access your camera and microphone. Click the Allow box and the close button to get started.

the Record button to start recording. Click the Stop button to finish. Once you do, you'll have the option to Reset and start again or Save what you recorded. To finish off the recording you need to complete a form that includes a title, the name of the people in the video, a description and privacy settings.

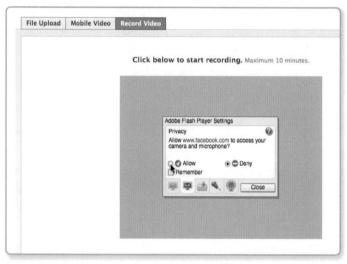

Above: Before you can record, you have to allow access to your camera and microphone.

GROUPS

To move outside of your immediate circle of friends use Facebook groups. These are based around a shared interest, hobby or cause and are as varied as the I Am Fluent In Sarcasm group and Anglo-Indian Cookery group. There are three types of groups:

- **Open (public)**: Anyone can join and can see the group postings.

- **Closed**: The group will show up in a search but you can't view any posts. You can ask to join but it is up to the administrator whether or not they accept you.

- **Secret groups**: These are not advertised on Facebook and you have to be invited to join.

Starting a Group

You can start your own group on any particular topic that interests you. Go to your home page and select Create Group from the Groups section in the left-hand pane. You will need to choose a name, add any members you want to invite and choose one of three possible privacy levels.

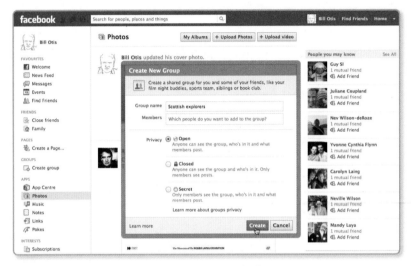

LISTS

Whereas groups have a shared space where, for example, a hockey team can share photos, lists are a way of organizing your friends and interests. These

Above: Before you start a new group, decide what privacy level to assign it.

lists are unique to you. You can, for example, create a list of work colleagues and only post items about your job to that list. Similarly, you could have a family list so that they are the only ones who get to know about your plans for a summer get together.

MAKE A LIST

To create a list go to your home page, select the MORE link next to Friends in the left-hand pane and click the + Create List. Write in the title of the list and any members you want to add, then click create. To speed up populating your list, click the title and add friends from the List suggestions shown on the right.

EVENTS

Facebook events are great for finding out what's going on as well as organising small get togethers or large-scale social gatherings.

See What's On

Upcoming events are listed on the right side of your home page, above the ads. To access the main page click the Events link in the left-hand pane.

Suggested Events

There may already be some suggested events, to which some of your friends are going. Use the search bar above to find others. If there's one that interests you, click the link for more details, information about who is attending, who's thinking of going and a button for you to join in.

Organizing Your Own

It's easy to organize your own event via Facebook.

1. Go to the Events page and click the + Create Event button. Fill in the information requested, the event name, date and time and location.

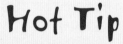

Hot Tip

If any of the guests you want at the event are not on Facebook you can email them an invite.

2. In the Details box you can add specific instructions for guests: directions, parking availability and so on.

3. Click the Guests button to display the Invite Friends box. Click the Add a Personal Message link if you want to add a more individual note.

    Right: Ensure you don't have unwanted guests at your event by checking the Invite only option to make it private.

Create new event

Name	Book signing
Details	The Return of Casablanca
Where	📍 Bury Street
When	19/8/2012 📅 19:30 UTC+01 End time?
Privacy	✉ Invite Only ▼ More Options

Invite friends   Create   Cancel

4. Choose whether you want the event to be public or private. Simply deselect the Make This Event Public to make it private (with young people this is a good idea, given the horror stories about teenagers advertising public parties on Facebook that have got out of control).

5. Check Show the Guest List if you want people to know who else has been invited.

6. Add a photo for the event, perhaps one of the venue or guest of honour, and click the Create Event button.

7. Having created the event you are automatically the administrator, so can change any details necessary, respond to questions and view who has replied.

ACCOUNT SETTINGS

There will be times when you want to access your Facebook account and make changes, such as enter a new password or a different email address. You can do so when you are logged into Facebook by clicking the downward-pointing arrow in the top navigation bar, then Account Settings. Choose the setting you want to change and click the Edit link to make them.

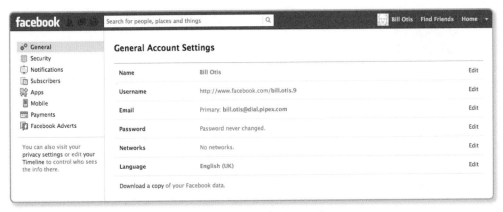

Above: You can change your password at any time by going to the Account Settings page.

Privacy Settings

Facebook does have quite extensive privacy settings, so use them. Go to the top navigation bar and click the downward-facing arrow, then select Privacy Settings.

Set the Default Privacy Setting

This is important, because it is the level of privacy that applies to any posts or photos you add to your timeline, if you don't set them individually. The choice is Public, Friends or Custom.

Hot Tip

Following concern about privacy and security on social networks, there are now more options for controlling these. When you edit each one there is an 'audience selector' that lets you choose who has access to you and your content.

APPS

Within Facebook itself there are a number of small apps – mini-programs – that do specific things. The photos app, for example, lets you create and organize your photos. In addition to the ones built-in to Facebook there are many apps available to add to the fun. Click on the App Centre in the left-hand pane on the home page and you'll see there are hundreds available. Just to give a flavour of some of the choice.

Left: Facebook will suggest different apps for you to try if are not sure of what's available.

⊜ **Social reading**: Newspapers like the *Guardian* will post the stories you read and videos you watch to your timeline, enabling you to share your views, if you wish, with your friends.

⊜ **Useful apps**: For remembering dates, such as MyCalendar for tracking birthdays or Quora, where you can ask questions and get answers posted to your timeline.

⊜ **Photo apps**: Like Instagram, which offers a fast, fun way to post photos and videos from your mobile to Facebook.

⊜ **Social games**: Like Draw Something where you draw a word while your friends guess what it is, or the popular FarmVille where you get to run your own farm.

Choosing Apps

To help you choose you can see a list of the apps your friends have used recently. There are also personalized suggestions from Facebook as well as links to the most popular and most used apps.

Using Apps

If you decide to add an app you have to give it permission to access your account. To do this, click the Allow button. These permissions can be edited at any time through your Apps Settings.

Mobile Facebook

Away from the computer doesn't mean out of touch. Facebook has its own mobile app that runs on smartphones like BlackBerry and iPhone and tablets such as the iPad. This gives you access to all the features you need to update your Timeline, add photos and videos, receive notifications, send messages and use your apps.

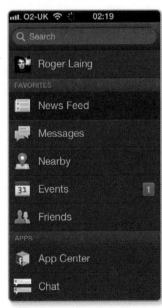

Above: FB's mobile app lets you update your Timeline wherever you are (pictured is Facebook on an iPhone).

LINKEDIN

As the primary social network for professionals, LinkedIn is designed to promote your career. It is based on making and managing professional contacts rather than the personal relationships that are central to Facebook.

LINKEDIN ACCOUNT TYPES

There are two types of Linkedin accounts.

- ➔ **Basic (free) account**: Fine for most users, it allows you to create a profile, build a professional network through your connections, get industry news and find and apply for jobs. You can always upgrade to a premium account.

- ➔ **Premium accounts**: There are various paid-for services that give you added features, such as seeing who has visited your profile page, additional ways of contacting people and, for jobseekers, the chance for your application to get pushed to the top of the pile.

STEP BY STEP: CREATE YOUR ACCOUNT

1. Enter your details in the Join Linkedin Today box and click the Join Now button.

2. Now start building your profile, which showcases your skills and experience. Fill in the details and click Create my profile.

3. Like any social network, LinkedIn offers to search your email contacts for people who are already members, as the fastest way to build up your network. If you want to do this fill in

your email password and press continue. Otherwise click Skip this step >>.

4. Next, LinkedIn needs to verify the email address you used to sign up for an account. Follow the prompts provided.

5. Once confirmed, LinkedIn is anxious for you to spread the news.

Above: Insert your details on-screen as prompted to join LinkedIn.

They offer to post a message of less than 140 characters, with a link to your profile, to Twitter and Facebook. As your profile is not complete it's best to click Skip this step>>.

6. It's still early to commit to a premium account but you can compare the benefits here and make your choice to arrive at your new Home page.

STEP BY STEP: GETTING STARTED

As with any social network, the first step once your account is open is to expand on your profile.

1. **Header:** Include details of your job title, location and industry.

2. **Professional headline:** Make this as full as possible so you stand out in search results.

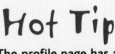

Hot Tip

The profile page has a bar that shows in percentage terms how complete your bio is and how to improve on this.

3. **Past position**: Used by LinkedIn to personalize its suggestions for potential connections as well as link you with former colleagues.

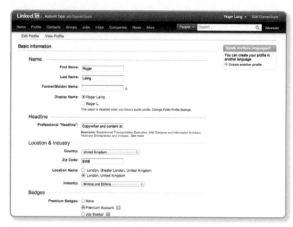

4. **Education**: So you can get in touch with other alumni who could be useful business contacts.

5. **Website**: Or your blog so people can find out more about you.

Above: Showcase your skills and experience by including as much information as you can on your profile.

6. **Twitter account**: So your LinkedIn connections can follow your tweets. Click the link and a popup window will appear asking you to login to Twitter.

7. **Enter Your Twitter Username & Password**: Then click Allow... LinkedIn doesn't actually store your password, so it's safe.

STEP BY STEP: ADD YOUR PROFILE PHOTO

As this is a professional social network, your photo should give a positive first impression.

1. Click Add Photo then Choose File. Find the photo you want on your hard drive and click Upload Photo.

2. A pop-up box will appear asking you to resize the image to focus on the area you want by moving and altering the yellow box.

3. When you're happy with the result click Save Photo then Save Settings.

KEEP UP TO DATE

LinkedIn is constantly redesigning the profile section to provide new ways for you to show your expertise. You can add new sections – such as patents you have or publications you have written. There are also applications you can add to your profile to link to blog articles, your creative portfolio and the like.

Hot Tip

To speed things up you can upload your CV (résumé). To be electronically readable it needs to be in a Word, PDF, Text or HTML format and be less than 500 KB in size. Just click the link beside Complete your profile quickly.

RECOMMENDATIONS

The LinkedIn equivalent of a reference, recommendations provide potential employers with a guide to the quality of your work and some evidence that you do have the experience you claim.

Select recommendations from the Profile link on the main navigation bar. Here you can request a recommendation, send one for someone else or manage those you've received. Mutual benefit means that it's often best when requesting a recommendation to offer one in exchange.

Revised recommendations

If you're not happy with the recommendation you can ask for a revised version. If they won't do that, or you're still dissatisfied, then you can hide it (although not delete it completely) by changing your display options. To do so, click Manage under the job title on the Received Recommendations tab.

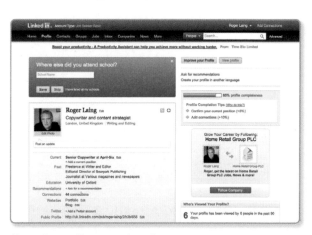

Above: Your profile page is what other users see, so ensure it is comprehensive and up-to-date.

CUSTOMIZE YOUR PUBLIC PROFILE

On your profile page you can choose which sections you want to make public. For example, you could choose to show your name and location, but not education details. Most users enable Full View, as this is likely to attract most new connections.

Hot Tip

The URL for your public profile is extremely unwieldy – it's not something you could easily add to your CV. To create your own, Click Edit then Customize your public profile URL and enter the name you want.

GET CONNECTED

There are many ways to add connections. To start, go to the Contacts link on the navigation bar and select Add Connections.

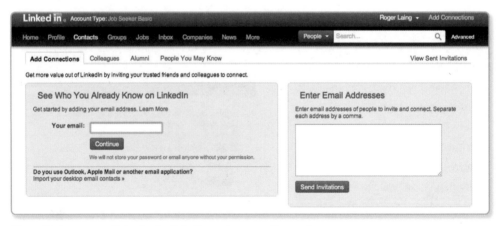

Above: Find contacts easily by allowing LinkedIn search your email account.

See Who You Already Know

This is the same box that's on your home page and that you'll have seen on sign-up. It will search your contacts book for possible connections.

➔ **Enter Email Addresses**: Lets you invite specific people, by entering their contact details and clicking the Send Invitations button.

➔ **Search**: Look for possible connections using the Search box in the top navigation bar. Make sure the type of search selector on the left is set to People. Click Advanced for a more sophisticated search where you can look for contacts according to company size, seniority and so on. In the tabbed menu at the top:

➔ **Colleagues**: This is the place to connect with people you work with now – and those you have known in the past.

➔ **Alumni**: These are potential connections based on the schools or universities listed in your profile.

➔ **People You May Know**: Personalized suggestions for new contacts based on your experience and existing network.

INVITATIONS

When you invite someone to connect they get a message in their LinkedIn inbox and will, typically, receive an email alert. It is always as well to include a little about yourself, even if you know them, to help jog their memory. They can accept your invitation, in which case you are both now part of each other's network, or ignore it.

THREE TIERS

Your LinkedIn network is made up of three tiers. How closely connected you are to another user is shown by a tiny degree icon:

➔ **Tier 1**: first-degree connections – your direct contacts, who either invited you to join their network or accepted an invitation to be part of yours.

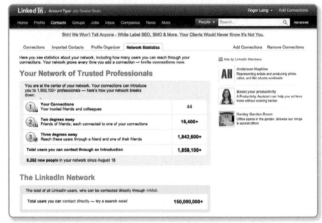

→ **Tier 2**: second-degree connections – friends of your friends, each of whom is connected to one of your connections.

→ **Tier 3**: third-degree connections – who are only linked directly to those in your second tier.

Above: The more contacts you have, the larger your possible network will be.

INMAIL

LinkedIn members inside and outside your network can also send a private message – known as InMail – direct to you. This is normally a premium feature.

FINDING A JOB

The quickest way to find a job is to use search in the top navigation bar, making sure the selector is set to jobs.

→ Click on the Advanced search link and you can filter jobs by location, experience, salary and more.

→ When you find one that looks right, click on the title to view the full description. Press the apply button to open an application form to which you can attach your CV and cover letter. If you're not quite ready you can save the job and come back to it later.

→ LinkedIn will also post a selection of Jobs you may be interested in, that match your LinkedIn profile, on your home page.

BE SELECTIVE

LinkedIn Today gives you the industry news you select in one place – on top of your home page. It can also be sent as a daily email.

1. Go to News on the navigation bar and select LinkedIn Today.

2. Select the industries you want to follow by clicking on Browse all >> in the header bar.

3. Click the Sources tab and choose which you want to show in your news feed.

4. Save your selection by clicking on Save Changes.

Hot Tip

Click on Network Statistics under the Contacts link on the navigation bar and you'll see the extraordinary number of professionals you can link to in each tier.

LINKEDIN MOBILE

As your career is too important to stay away from for long, there are mobile apps for BlackBerry, iPhone or iPad, Android smartphone or tablet as well as access on any Internet-ready mobile at http://touch.linkedin.com.

Right: LinkedIn viewed on a mobile.

GOOGLE+

Although known primarily as the company behind the search engine, Google is a big social media player through YouTube and Blogger. Google+ is its version of a social network to rival Facebook.

WHAT IS GOOGLE+?

As the latest entrant to social networking, Google+ isn't the biggest, but it is growing rapidly. While it has many of the same features as Facebook – the Stream (News Feed on Facebook) of multimedia posts from Circles (Groups on Facebook) of friends – it does seem to be appealing more to business users. It also has one advantage that Facebook can't compete with – it is closely integrated with all Google's other services.

USING GOOGLE+

The link between Google+ and the company's other services is such that you access it through your Google account. If you have Gmail, or use another service like Reader or Google Docs, you will have an account. If not, it's easy – and free – to sign up. Go to http://accounts.google.com.

Above: To access Google+, you need to have a Google Account.

To access your Google+ account, go to the black navigation bar at the top of any Google service and click +Yourname. You'll be guided through the account activation process.

→ This will include your public profile. As usual, you will be asked to add a photo, give details of where you live, work and were educated.

CIRCLES

You will also be asked if you'd like to add people you know to Circles. These are like Groups on Facebook, but they control much more of what you see and share. You put the people you know into circles based on the relationship you have with them. So you might have different circles for family, business colleagues, old university friends, work friends, work colleagues, best friends and so on. Although you add them to your circle, they don't have to reciprocate.

→ To organize your Circles, click the icon in the navigation panel. You'll see all the people in your circles, which may be those you created or predefined by Google+.

→ Click the Find people tab and you'll see suggestions of who to add, including those in your contacts book who are already members. When you've found someone to add simply drag their photo to a Circle.

→ They'll get a notification from Google+ but won't know the name of the Circle (fortunate if they're placed in the annoying family members' circle) and won't know if they're ever removed.

→ Google+ will also suggest interesting and famous people whose posts you may like to follow. As you are only following them, none of your posts will be sent to their Stream.

Right: You can choose which Circles the people you know are added to.

YOUR STREAM

This is your home page, similar to the News Feed in Facebook. It shows all the postings from your Circles of friends and followers and your posts.

Above: You are able to join in with discussions that are trending on Google+ by clicking on the link that interests you.

- Click on any of the Trending on Google+ feed to see the hot stories from across the network.

- On the left side is the navigation panel. Click on the icon to go to that page. As this is Google there is a large Search bar at the top. On the far right is Google Chat – Google's instant messaging service.

CREATING POSTS

When you want to post to your Stream, click the box that has the words Share what's new. Alternatively, if you're on other pages, click the +Share button beside your profile photo. The box expands and you can type in your message. You can add photos, videos, an event or a link by clicking the relevant icon below the box.

SHARING

Google+ allows you to be much more targeted in terms of who you share your messages with.

- The Share box is pre-populated with a couple of suggestions: Friends and Business. If you don't want these click the small x in the corner to remove them.

- Click on +Add more people and you can include your choice of circles. To add individual names click the Browse people icon (the head with + sign).

In addition to selecting who sees the post, you can control how they respond. You can prevent other people adding their thoughts to your post by clicking the small downward-pointing arrow in the sharing box and selecting Disable Comments. Alternatively, Lock This Post stops anyone who receives it from sharing it with people who weren't on your original list.

When ready, click the Share button and your post will appear in the Streams of the people you choose, plus your own. If comments are allowed they will show up under that post and you'll be sent an alert.

JOIN THE SLOW STREAM

Your Stream can get quite confusing, as it shows everyone's posts by default. You can filter this to just show individual Circles by selecting the one you want from the Stream header at the top of the page. For instance, clicking the Friends button will just show posts from that Circle. The rest of the Timeline is taken up with stories and photos grouped by date and year.

Above: Too much information? To filter your Stream, click on the Friends button to see posts only from that Circle.

GOOGLE +1

The +1 buttons are similar to the Like button in Facebook. Clicking the button, which you see at the bottom of every post, shows that you like it without having to add a comment. The writer of the post will get a notification that you like it.

Like It, +1 It

These +1 buttons are also on sites all over the web. Click one and it will be shown on the +1 tab on your profile page. If you've made this publicly visible, it gives people browsing your profile a better idea of your likes and interests.

Above: By +1-ing something, you can recommend it to others in your circles.

You can also make it work as a bookmark. When you come across a site you want to return to, such as a display of vintage maps, click the +1 button and the link will appear in the +1s on your profile.

REPOSTING

Just like Twitter's retweet, reposting lets you share a post with your Circles. Just press the Share link (the right-pointing arrow icon) under the post to send a copy to your Stream. The amount of activity around a post is shown at the bottom. Click the link and you can see the names of those who have +1'd the post and shared it. Hover your mouse over their name and beside their picture is an Add button if you want to invite them to join your circles.

HANGOUTS

Sometimes, rather than just add a comment on a post, you'd like to make your point face-to-face. Do so with video chat. Click the movie camera icon to Start a hangout about this post.

How to Hangout

The first time you may be asked to install a plug-in. This will set up the toolbar to control your hangout. From here you can invite people, start a chat, share a video and attach headwear, like pirate hats or fake moustaches to everyone. A strip of thumbnail-sized video pictures of everyone in the hangout is shown along the bottom. When someone talks, their picture is pushed up to the main screen.

Keep in Touch

Hangouts are a great way to keep in touch with friends and family, wherever they live or to hold virtual business meetings. Up to 10 people can hangout at once, for free and for businesses there are live broadcast options too. Click the Hangouts icon on the navigation bar and you can see some of the upcoming hangouts to join.

PHOTOS

When you click on the Photo link there's a range of options. You can create an album, use your webcam to take a shot and add files from your computer, Google Drive or mobile using Instant Upload. You can access your photos in two separate places, either through the Photos tab on your profile page or by clicking the Photos icon on the navigation bar. Here you can organize any profile photos you have and albums, as well as see photos from your posts or where you have been tagged. You can also invite others to view particular albums.

VIDEOS

Any videos you add will show up on the video tab on your profile page. They can then be managed in much the same way as your photos.

EVENTS

Instead of posting a thought or a message you can create an event from within your Stream by choosing the Event icon. This could be for a hangout or a real-world celebration.

Above: Google+ allows you to create invites to send to chosen friends, even if they aren't Google+ users.

INVITES

There are pre-set themes to decorate your invites and room for all the information about time, location and so on. Events can be seen and replied to through Google Calendar. You can allow guests to invite others, if you want, and to add their photos, direct from the event, so they are all available in one place.

BLOGGING

WHAT IS BLOGGING?

Whether it's a quick thought you want to share – or long-held personal views – blog about it. Blogs and bloggers are the new social commentators, often rivalling major media companies as a source of information.

JOIN THE BLOGOSPHERE

There are more than 120 million active blogs (the word comes from weblogs) being tracked across the Internet. People love to have a place online where they can have their say.

SPEAK YOUR MIND

The blogosphere – as blogs are collectively known – is still largely (60 per cent) for hobbyists, according to Technorati, the blog search engine. Bloggers don't plan to make money from their blog; their satisfaction comes from being able to speak their minds.

Photos, amusing posts, links: the more you add to your blog, the more hits you are likely to receive.

WHY BLOG?

There are many reasons why people blog; these are some:

→ **Blogging for fun**: The chance to share your world view and let your personality – or that of your subject – shine through. For example, Funny or Snot (www.funnyorsnot.com).

→ **Blogging about an interest**: Like gadgets? Blog about it and you get to enjoy your hobby and meet people that share your interest. For example, Macrumors (www.macrumours.com) for Apple enthusiasts.

➔ **Blogging to make a name for yourself**: Celebrities, authors, sports people and the like blog about their work to get more recognition and build their audience. For example, author David Hewson (www.davidhewson.com).

➔ **Blogging for business**: Lets you share knowledge and expertise to boost sales and promote your business, both directly and indirectly. For example, Workshifting (www.workshifting.com) is a blog by Citrix Online promoting the idea that 'anywhere is my office'.

WHAT SORT OF BLOG?

You are the publisher, so it is up to you what content is on your blog. Below are some of the main categories, but there's often overlap.

Personal

Written by you, about you – your likes, dislikes, events in your life, family, hobbies or whatever motivates you.

Business

There's a commercial aim – sharing knowledge to highlight why you are the right company to do business with.

Corporate

These are the blogs of big enterprises. With less of a sales pitch than a business blog, the intent is similar, to show your value as a commercial partner.

Non-profit

An essential part of fund-raising for many causes, blogs not only highlight where help is urgently needed, but also show how donations are used.

Hot Tip

Blogs have come a long way from their origins as a personal online diary. Now it's easy to add audio and video as well as photos, messages, illustrations, links and more.

Above: Microlocal media: these blogs enable stories that wouldn't otherwise hit the headlines to be reported on locally.

News

Hyperlocal (or microlocal media) is news about a small area or locality, which can be supported by selling advertising to local businesses.

Expert

If you have a particular expertise, share it. Those that do, value the feedback they get on their ideas through their blog, as well as the professional opportunities that follow.

Fanzines

If you follow a local sports team, blog about it and capture the interest of fellow enthusiasts. If it's not sport, Creating a blog around one of the celebrities you like or music, films, TV shows, theatre, dance – any form of entertainment you enjoy.

Niche

However particular your interest, the one place you are likely to find others that share it is on the web. Start your blog and see who follows.

BLOGGING DOS

⊙   **Do be yourself**: What makes blogs different to every other medium is that it is your personality that's on show.

⊙   **Do attribute content you use**: If you quote someone, or use content from their blog, give them a credit and a link. This not only avoids any problems of plagiarism, but also helps your blog's search engine rankings.

⊙   **Do include images**: Perfect as your words are, visitors like pictures.

→ **Do comment on comments**: When someone takes the trouble to comment it's good to reply and start a conversation. That won't happen if you simply thank them for the comment, as some recommend.

→ **Do use social media**: Like Facebook, Twitter and LinkedIn to push readers to your blog.

BLOGGING DON'TS

→ **Don't set music or videos to auto-play**: However much you like the tune, or laugh at the video of your cat falling off the windowsill.

→ **Don't write long posts**: Because you can't be bothered to edit your thoughts and create shorter ones.

→ **Don't forget you have a spellcheck**: You don't want anything, however trivial, to put readers off.

→ **Don't make it too difficult to add comments**: You have to balance precautions to stop spammers against killing feedback.

→ **Don't give up**: OK, so you haven't ranked No. 1 on Google yet, but don't despair, it takes time to build an audience.

Above: This mobile app (viewed here on an iPhone) allows you to post away to your heart's content, wherever you are.

MOBILE BLOGGING

Many of us read blogs on mobile devices every day. Now there are plenty of apps that let you post to your blog. Take a photo at an event or on a trip, type a few lines of commentary and use a wireless or mobile connection to publish it to the web, instantly.

MICROBLOGGING WITH TWITTER

These mini blogs, where posts are very short, make it quick and easy to tell people what's happening in your world, right now. The best-known microblogging site is Twitter.

WHAT IS MICROBLOGGING?

Microblogging is like blogging, except the posts are much shorter. In the case of the best-known site, Twitter, updates have to be 140 characters or fewer, including spaces. These posts can be posted for anyone to see, or to a selected group chosen by the user.

HOW IT DIFFERS FROM BLOGGING

The most obvious difference is the length of the posts. Updates are restricted in length on microblogging sites, whereas you have room to write as much as your readers can stand on a blog. Updates are also quicker, near-instant, on microblogging sites, and can be sent directly to other users you choose.

Above: Tweets posted on Twitter range from the sublime to the ridiculous, and everything in between.

INTRODUCING TWITTER

Twitter is a web-based messaging service. Initially it was designed for you to send quick and frequent updates to the question: 'What are you doing?', and it is still used that way. People share what they had for their breakfast, along with their news, opinions and jokes. But it has also since emerged as an international reporting tool, with Twitter breaking the news of the terrorist attacks in Mumbai. In addition it an be a campaigning tool for politicians and causes, a marketing tool for companies and much more. The joy of Twitter that takes it beyond just being an instant messaging service, is that you can follow whoever you want and anyone can follow you.

Above: Picture 1: complete the form.

STEP BY STEP: CREATE AN ACCOUNT ON TWITTER

1. Go to www.twitter.com and complete the form (*see* Picture 1).

2. Click Sign up and on the following page you will choose your username, or 'Twitter handle'. Be sure you're happy with it, as this is your personal brand.

Above: Picture 2: choose your username and Twitter handle. .

3 Twitter will suggest a username for you with further suggestions in green beneath. Overwrite this with your choice and Twitter will let you know if it's available (*see* Picture 2).

4. To encourage you to get started, Twitter will show a list of the most popular Tweeters (the Twitterati) to follow; suggest interests that might match yours; or search your contacts (*see* Picture 3).

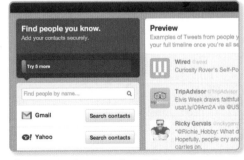

Above: Picture 3: you can choose whether or not Twitter searches your email account for possible contacts.

5. Skip these options for now and click the Create my account button. Check your email account for the confirmation email and reply to activate your account.

> ## Hot Tip
>
> **Make your username short, 12 characters or less, so people can mention you in their tweets without running out of space.**

SETTING UP YOUR PROFILE

Once you've opened your account, filling in your profile will increase the chances that people who see your tweets will want to follow you. This is also the information that will appear in your public profile and in search results on Twitter and the web. To start, click your username above the View My Profile Page link in the box on the left then click the Edit your profile button.

↪ **Picture:** Add a photo, to show you're a real person. Twitter lore says that no one wants to follow an egg – the default image used for new accounts.

↪ **Name:** This sits next to your Twitter handle, so if you've shortened that to reduce the character length, spell it out in full now.

↪ **Location:** This improves the chances of being returned in a search and let's people know where you are based.

↪ **Website:** Link to your blog, personal website or LinkedIn profile.

↪ **Bio:** Good practice for your tweets. The challenge is to describe yourself and what you'll be blogging about in less than 160 characters.

↪ **Facebook:** Click the link for your Twitter tweets to be simultaneously posted as your Facebook status.

Once your profile is set up, click the
Save button.

FOLLOWING

When you first sign up, Twitter suggests
people to follow and continues to do so in
the Who to Follow box on the left of your
home page.

Meet The Rich & Famous

Click the Browse categories link in the Who to
Follow box and select an area that interests
you, such as Entertainment. This takes you to
a list of suggested people to follow – such as
Jim Carrey, Ashton Kutcher or Oprah Winfrey.
If the category is Fashion, it will include
companies like Yves Saint Laurent as well as
individuals like Kim Kardashian. Each
suggestion includes the user's picture, profile
and a brief description. Click on any of these
areas and the user's latest tweets appear in a
pop-up window.

Following Along

You can also see how many times they've
tweeted, how many followers they have
(including how many of the people you
follow are also following them) and how
many they are following. To join their list

Above: Complete your profile page once you've set up
your account.

Hot Tip

**Your Twitter page doesn't have to be
the default blue clouds. Click Design
in your profile and you can change
to one of the ready-made themes.
Alternatively, you can personalize it
with your own background image
and colours.**

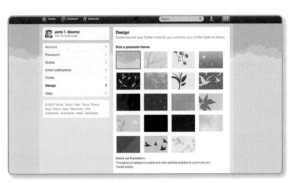

Above: Customize your Twitter page to make it stand out.

Hot Tip

How do you know you're looking at the real account of the star? Beside the name, you'll see a white tick inside a blue circle. This shows that their identity has been verified and that they really are who they say they are.

simply click the Follow button with the blue Twitter bird icon, which will change to say Following.

Finding People You Know

Click the Find friends link in the Who to follow box. Here you can search your webmail contacts, like Gmail or Yahoo!, to see if any are already on Twitter. You can then choose to follow them. If there are particular people you want to join your network, simply enter their addresses in the Invite friends to Twitter via email text box and click the button.

Search for People

The box at the top of the main content area lets you locate people on Twitter by their real name (Gordon Ramsay) or Twitter username (GordonRamsay01), as well as search for a particular topic, such as TV chefs.

Above: To follow someone, simply search for their name, select it, and click Follow.

Finding Other People to Follow

There are several ways to expand the list of people you follow on Twitter.

→ **Your followers' followers:** Look at their tweets to see whom they are chatting with, shown by @username. Click that link and see if it's someone you want to follow.

→ **Look for twitter names:** Either from blogs that you like, articles or events. Many people also include their Twitter handle on other social media, such as Facebook or LinkedIn.

Follow hashtags (#) at events: For many events, organizers will create and publicize a hashtag (for example, #edfringe for the hundreds of comedy, theatre and music shows put on at the annual Edinburgh Festival Fringe in Scotland). Anyone tweeting from the event can use that hashtag. Search Twitter for it and you can see all the people who are there, even if you don't follow them.

Above: Hashtags are a way of organizing tweets on a certain topic.

Getting People to Follow You

Twitter is great for making contact with people you would never probably have the chance to meet in the real world, for simple reasons of location and so on. Having made the contact, it can only develop if the people you follow return the compliment. There are ways to increase your chances of being followed.

Improve your profile: People will look at this and past tweets to make a decision about whether to follow you.

Reply to any tweets that mention you: But try to move the conversation forward, rather than simply thanking them for including your name.

Comment on tweets and retweet the good ones: It's flattering to have your tweet picked up and sent around the twittersphere, provided it's for positive reasons. If you've retweeted to pour scorn on someone, you're unlikely to gain a follower.

TWEETING

To send a tweet, go to your home page. You can either click the tweet box on the left-hand side marked Compose New Tweet... or click on the feather pen and paper icon on the header bar to open a text box, labelled What's happening? Start typing your message and four new elements appear:

- **Camera icon**: Click this to attach images to your tweet.

- **Compass icon**: Add your location to your tweet. This will turn on the feature for all future tweets, although you'll have the option to switch it off before sending individual tweets.

- **140**: Shows how many of the maximum 140 characters for each tweet (including spaces) that you have left.

- **Tweet button**: Click this to send your tweet.

Above: Want to tweet? Simply click in the Compose New Tweet box on your home page.

Sending Your Tweet

Once you send your tweet it will appear on your home timeline along with all those from Twitter users you follow. The newest updates will be at the top. Hover over a Tweet and you'll see the links to Expand the message, Reply, Retweet or add it as a Favorite. This last option adds the tweet to a list of your favourites that can be accessed later through your profile page.

ADDING TO A TWEET

There are various options to add extra value to your tweet.

Links

Include URLs and links to other pages, such as a blog or website. Find the link you want and paste it into your tweet window. Twitter will automatically shorten it so it uses only 20 characters. It will start with t.co.

Hot Tip

You can click anywhere on a tweet to expand it so you can see photos, videos and other information.

Hashtags

A way of grouping all tweets on a particular topic or event, so you can view them in one place. The hashtag symbol (#) is placed immediately before a word or phrase with no spaces.

- ➔ Click a hashtag and you'll see all other tweets on that topic in chronological order. Regular hashtags you'll see include #ff – Follow Friday. This is an end-of-the-working-week list that users make of those they follow and find particularly interesting.

- ➔ If you're tweeting about a topic that lots of others are writing about, use the same hashtag for your tweets, for example #Olympics. When anyone searches for that hashtag, they will see all the tweets on that topic, with yours among them.

- ➔ The most popular hashtagged words become trending topics, which are shown in the Trends box on your home page. Whichever one you click will show all the tweets on that topic.

Above: Go to bit.ly to shorten URLs that may be too long to tweet.

RETWEETS

When you see an interesting tweet, you can send it to your followers, that is retweet it. You can send it as it is, or add your own comment. The easiest way to retweet is to hover over a tweet and click the Retweet link that appears. You should leave the letters RT in the tweet to show it is retweeted. There's some kudos gained if your tweets are retweeted by others. You can see your retweets by clicking @ Connect on the main navigation bar and then selecting Interactions.

> ## Hot Tip
> Trends are based on your location and who you follow, so as to make them relevant to you. If you'd prefer to see what's trending elsewhere, click **Change** in the Trends box and choose a different location.

Above: Retweeting is a great way of sharing interesting tweets with your followers.

REPLY

To keep the conversation going you can reply to an interesting tweet. Hover over the tweet and click the reply icon. In the box that opens you'll see it has the @username of the person you're replying to. Complete your message and click Tweet to send.

MENTIONS

If you include someone's username (for example, @BillGates for the founder of Microsoft) anywhere within a tweet it appears in that person's timeline (even if they do not follow you). Depending on what you say, this could be a good way of introducing yourself to people who are not followers. The more celebrated they are, however, the less likely they are to reply.

DIRECT MESSAGES

You can only send a private tweet to someone who follows you, although you can receive a direct message from anyone you follow. To send your message, click the drop-down menu beside the person icon on the header bar and select Direct Messages.

Above: Including a non-follower's username in a tweet is a subtle way of getting them to follow you.

PHOTOS

Twitter is still largely a text-based system, so while it's possible to include photos, these are links that will send you to a separate webpage rather than part of the message. To add a photo, click the Camera icon in the tweet box. Currently, Twitter only allows 1 image per tweet, which has to be less than 3 MB in size.

VIDEOS

While Twitter is happy for you to share videos, it is not as easy as including a photo. Twitter itself doesn't host videos, so you have to use outside systems. Most of these, like YouTube and Vimeo (vimeo.com), have a button on their site that lets you post the video direct to Twitter, by including it as a link.

When you expand the tweet these videos will appear, so users can watch them without leaving their timeline. If the video is not on any of the supported sites, you can still cut and paste the video link into your Tweet.

Above: Sites such as this allow you to compose longer tweets.

BREAK THE LIMITS

It may seem against the spirit of the game, but there are ways round Twitter's 140 character limit. You can, and some do, send a series of tweets that the recipients then have to stitch together. As a more polished alternative, there are services that will take your tweet, include a link within the 140-character limit and display the rest on an external website. Among them are www.jumbotweet.com and, for the more commercially minded, www.longrep.ly.

PRIVACY

Part of the attraction of Twitter is that anyone can read your tweets, whether they are followers or not. Despite that, you can create a closed group. Go to Settings in the drop-down menu beside the person icon and click Account. Scroll down and select the option Protect My Tweets. Any future tweets will now only be visible to your followers, who will have to ask to be part of the group. They won't be able to retweet any of your updates.

LISTS

When you have lots of tweets on a particular topic of interest and want to organize them, you can create a list. To do so go to your profile page, select Lists then click the Create list button.

Organizing Your Tweets in Lists

Enter a name for your list that is 25 characters or fewer and a short description. You can make it private – only accessible by you – or public where anyone can subscribe and follow your list.

Subscribe to a List

If you admire someone else's list you can subscribe to it, just like following a user.
When looking at the person's profile, click on the Lists tab and select the one that interests
you. On the List page click Subscribe to follow the list.

MOBILE TWITTER

Designed for its immediacy, it's not surprising that most people use Twitter on the go, through
their mobiles, smartphone and tablets. Not only has Twitter created mobile applications for the
different platforms, but there are also a host of third-party programs for using Twitter on the go.

TweetDeck

This is a downloadable application,
which can help you manage many
of your social media accounts, not
just Twitter. You can use it to view
and post to multiple accounts at
once. This is especially useful if
you have more than one Twitter
account plus a Facebook and
LinkedIn account. TweetDeck
allows you to write your message
once and post in all sites instantly,
or just one at a time. Go to
www.tweetdeck.com.

Above: The HootSuite app for the iPad lets you view several of
your Twitter feeds at a time.

HootSuite

Similar to TweetDeck, HootSuite also lets you schedule your tweets in advance, so they go out
on a specific date at a certain time. HootSuite also manages several Twitter accounts together.
Go to www.hootsuite.com.

HOSTED BLOGS

If you want to concentrate on the content in your blog and not worry about the technology that's needed to run it, then you want a hosted blog.

WHAT IS A HOSTED BLOG?

Blogs today are quite sophisticated. They are complete content management systems for users to write, edit and store and publish their blog online, including text, pictures and video. They need to look beautiful, be simple to use yet support reader comments, links and subscriptions and much more. Fortunately, there's software that does most of the hard work, but this has to be housed somewhere. These hosted blogs are usually provided by the companies that make the blogging software, like WordPress, Blogger and TypePad. They'll take care of the software so you can concentrate on the content.

Hosted Blog Services

Typically, hosted blogging plans will include free, basic accounts with extra, premium features which are chargeable, such as more storage, no ads and video embedding.

→ **Xanga (www.xanga.com):**
Combines blogging with social networking. Although there's space to publish text, photos, audio and video on your own blog, it relies more than other sites on members' interaction. The home page shows the top blog posts along with a range of special interest blog communities – such as for health or food – that you can join.

Hot Tip

Write down a list of what's most important for your blog before you compare hosts. For example, ad income may be nice to have but not vital, whereas having your own URL might be essential.

Blogger (www.blogger.com): One of the first blogging applications, Blogger remains very popular, in part because it's free. Owned by Google it links to their other services. For example, images you use go to your Picasa web album, which is also free (although there is a chargeable upgrade option if you want more storage space). Blogger is easily customizable, has a reasonable range of features, and you can make money by publishing Google ads.

Above: Why not join a blogging community, such as Xanga?

WordPress (www.wordpress.com): Sister to the DIY-hosted product. The free version comes with limited features: there are a restricted choice of design templates unless you pay to upgrade. It is, however, very easy to get your blog up and running. It does include some very useful features, such as automatic pinging of blog search sites to announce your new blog post and plug-ins to stop spam.

TypePad (www.typepad.com): Has traditionally placed a big emphasis on easy design and maintenance. While there are many ways to customize and extend your TypePad blog, such as having more than one blog and several authors, it may mean upgrading to a more expensive package.

Above: WordPress is a free and easy way to get your blog up and running with paid-for features available if you need them.

SETTING UP A BASIC BLOG

While hosted blogs differ in the features they offer – and the price – they mostly operate in similar ways. Here, as an example, we are using the TypePad Plus account.

STEP BY STEP: CREATING AN ACCOUNT

1. To start your journey to the blogosphere, go to www.typepad.com, click on the Start Now button then on the Sign Up 14 day free trial.

2. Enter the information requested. The first big choice is your blog URL. Like most hosted blog services, the basic URL with your TypePad account will be in the format yourblogname.typepad.com. You want to make it something short but memorable. It also has to be unique, so don't be surprised if it takes several attempts to find a name that's available.

3. Once the details are complete, you'll see the 'Congratulations, you have a TypePad Blog!' message. Click the Get Started! button.

4. If you want to get started right away, you can choose to write your first post or style the design of your site. If not, you can start customizing your blog.

5. As you can have more than one blog, the first thing to do is select the right one from the drop-down list on the top navigation bar. By default it will be called My Blog. On the Overview tab you can see recent activity on your site,

Hot Tip

If you want to use your own domain name for your blog, such as www.myadventuresinblogland.com, you can do this later using the domain mapping option.

where the traffic – visitors – are coming from and so on. For the moment, there's not much happening here.

SETTINGS

To get the maximum impact from your blog, you need to set it up to work the way you want. Below are some of the settings you can configure to get your blog to work the way you want.

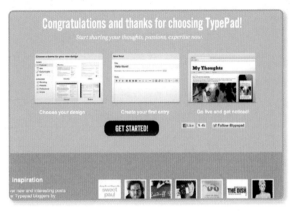

Above: As there's no software to set up, hosted blogs do have advantages for the user over DIY blogs.

Basic Settings

Basic they may be but these settings are important. Start with your Blog Name and Blog Description. These can be changed when you want, but they do need some thought to get them both punchy and descriptive.

- **Blog folder**: This is where your blog files will be stored. It will also appear at the end of your URL.

- **Private blog**: Select Password if you want your blog to be private, only accessible by those who know the password. While this runs contrary to the nature of a blog, where most bloggers want their blogs to be seen and commented on, you may want to use this while you're setting the site up or during a redesign.

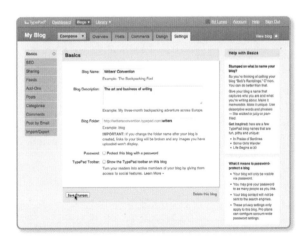

Above: Changing the name of your blog folder may cause you problems.

SEO Settings

SEO stands for search engine optimization. These settings are designed to make it more likely that your blog is picked up by search engines, and if it is that it has a higher ranking in search results than similar blogs.

> # Hot Tip
> **While you can change the name of your blog folder, any previous links you've set up won't work if you do.**

→ **Publicity**: Select the Publicize This Blog box.

→ **Google Sitemap**: This creates a sitemap of your blog, which makes it more likely Google will index your blog and send traffic to it.

→ **Meta keywords**: Like the Meta description – makes up your blog's metadata. This is 'data about data', information that doesn't appear on your blog pages but is in the code and can be read by search engines. Pay particular attention to the Meta Description as this is the text that's put after the link to your blog on search engine results.

Above: Linking your blog to other social media will increase your readership.

Sharing Settings

Add the popular Facebook Like icon to your blog here, so readers can share their appreciation with their Facebook friends. You can also link your blog to many of your social media accounts, such as Facebook, Twitter, FriendFeed and others. This includes automatically updating Facebook and Twitter when you publish a new blog post.

Feeds Settings

People who like your site can subscribe, via a feed or email, so they are automatically alerted when there's new content and won't miss anything. The settings here also let you connect to Feedburner, which will help you set up and manage your feed.

Add-ons Settings

It's good to know who's coming to your site, what posts they're reading, how long they're spending and so on. Fortunately, Google Analytics will tell you all this and more, for free. You first have to set up an account with Google, which is easily done by going to www.google.com/analytics. They will give you a unique tracking code, a UA number, which has to be put on every

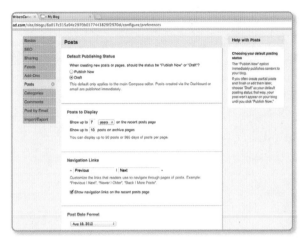

Above: Buy yourself some time to read your post over before publishing it by clicking on Draft in the Default Publishing Status settings.

page of your blog. You only need to add it once, in the Google Analytics box on the Add-ons page and it will be automatically posted throughout your site.

Posts Settings

However confident a writer you are, you don't want to publish a post until you're sure you are ready. In Posts settings you can set the Default Publishing Status to Draft. That way whenever you save a post it will not be published on the live site but kept for you to review again later.

- **Posts to Display**: Lets you select how many posts to have on your home page. You don't want too many or people will have to scroll down a very long page. Nor do you want too few or it looks as though there's little content on the site. A good average is five to seven posts.

- **Front Page Heading**: Lets you choose whether you have a traditional blog, with the most recent posts on your home page or, like a website, with a static page where the home page stories remain the same.

Categories Settings

The best way of organizing your content so readers can search your site for posts on the topics that interest them. This will become more important as your blog grows. The Categories settings allow you to edit and delete them. As you saw above, you can also create new categories as you add individual posts.

Above: Discourage unwanted visitors by checking the boxes in the Unauthenticated Commenters section in Comments settings.

Comments Settings

While you want to encourage a conversation with your visitors, you also need to discourage spam. If it's too restrictive to get people to register before they comment, you should tick the Require an Email Address and Require Readers to Enter a Randomly Generated Verification Code under the Unauthenticated Commenters heading. You should also moderate comments. Select Yes, Hold Comments for My Approval and you have the chance to review and delete any spam messages before they are published to the blog and annoy other users.

Turn on Comment Sharing and Facebook Comment Syncing so your readers can share your posts on other social media sites as well as synchronize any comments on your blog with their Facebook updates.

YOUR PROFILE

As always in social media, one of the first steps is to put your character on your blog by completing your profile. To do so click your name on the navigation bar and then Edit Your Profile in the left-hand panel.

● **Change your URL**: Using the keyword or phrase that best describes your blog, so it will be picked up by search engines.

● **Enter your one line bio**: One line says it all. To say more, use the About Me page. This is where people who are interested in your blog will go if they do want to find out more about you.

● **Click the Choose File button**: To find your photo of choice to attach to your profile. Then click save.

DESIGN

Arguably, as important as what you say is how you choose to display it. If your site looks amateurish and poorly designed, your words have to work twice as hard to change that impression.

Above: The look of your blog is very important, so play around with different ideas before finalizing it.

● Go to the Dashboard, then select the Design link in the Manage My Blog panel. Click the Choose a theme... button and scroll through the links to find the one that appeals to you. Press the Choose a theme... button again and then Save Changes if you want to apply the new design to your blog.

Hot Tip

Want to see how your blog will look in each theme? Click the Preview button.

Layout

Within the Design section, click the Layouts link to choose whether your blog has one, two, three or four columns.

Organizing Your Blog

There are certain features – content modules – like the archives, search box and so on, which you can move around the layout. On the Design page, click the link to Content and scroll through the list of modules to see which you want to add. To move a module once it's added, simply drag and drop it in the sidebar in the order you prefer. Again use the Preview button to see the effect of the changes.

Post

Central to the blog are your posts and TypePad makes publishing them easy. On the Dashboard, click the Write a full post >> link in the Quick Post panel. In the New Post box enter a title and your update. You'll see there's a ribbon of icons, just like the ones used in word-processing programs, which allow you to format your content, change the font etc.

On the right-hand side choose the category for this post. You can add new categories if you've not yet set them up. Each post can be added to several categories.

Under the post itself expand the Comments and Trackbacks section to make sure they are both marked Open. This means readers can comment on your posts and any other sites that are linking back to your post will be displayed.

Above: You can decide how the elements of the page should be organized and preview it before anything is finalized.

Enter the relevant keywords: These are the main words or phrases that summarize the topic you're writing about, such as stained glass design, as well as the tags for Technorati, the blog search engine.

Share the post: With your friends on other social media, so your Facebook and Twitter status will be updated when you publish a new post.

Feature this post: While posts are usually shown in the order they were published, if there's one that's particularly important, you can tick the box in this section to keep it at the top of your home page.

Above: Save your post as Draft if you want to check it before publishing.

When you're ready, click the drop-down menu next to status. Select whether you want to publish your post immediately, at some specified date in the future or save it as a draft.

PREMIUM FEATURES

On some hosted plans, there is a basic free account and other premium features that are available to anyone for a fee. These extras may be more storage space (so you can have a bigger site, or several sites); extra monthly bandwidth (for bigger uploads and to support more traffic); greater customization (such as a wider range of themes and use of your own domain name); or enhanced features (like video support, anti-spam controls and eCommerce plug-ins so you can sell things through your blog). On other hosted blog services, like TypePad, the features available depend on the plan you buy. To access more advanced features you may have to upgrade your account.

DIY BLOGS

Although it seems daunting at first, it is possible for the non-technical person to set up and run their own blog. If you do get into problems, there are many people who can help.

BENEFITS OF A DIY BLOG

The main advantage of hosting your own blog is the freedom it offers. You have greater choice over the look and feel of your site. You can choose what features to have – like your own ads – as well as what not to have – the service provider's ads that come with many free hosted accounts. You can also run your blog as part of your website rather than keep the two separately.

CHOOSING A WEB HOST

With freedom comes responsibility. The first decision is choosing your web host. In a way DIY hosting, or self-hosting as it is also called, is a bit misleading. In reality, someone else is still hosting your blog, providing the physical storage space, computer power and connection to the Internet. You just manage it. Here are some points to consider when it comes to choosing a host.

Above: There are many possible web hosts, so don't opt for the first one you find.

→ **Price**: And what you get for it. It is a really competitive market, so shop around.

→ **Space**: While this won't be an issue starting off, it could be later when it would be very difficult to move. With large photos, audio files and increasingly videos on blogs, the requirements for storage space are rapidly increasing. Aim for more than you think you need.

Data transfer and bandwidth: A great area of confusion. Web host providers will often talk about bandwidth or bandwidth limit with what seems to be an impressively high number. This is, in effect, the size of the tube that they allow for getting everything to and from your server. This figure will not change. What does change is the data transfer rate, also called monthly traffic, monthly transfer limit and so on. This is the amount of information – pictures, files, audio, video and so on – transferred from your server when visitors look at your blog or when you are setting up the pages. It will also vary according to the number of visitors you have and what they view on the site. This 'traffic' figure is often limited and is the one to use to compare different web hosting plans. Most hosts do offer upgrade plans.

Reliability and uptime: It's easy to get baffled by the claims – 99.95 per cent, 98 per cent uptime – that is the percentage of time the server holding your blog is available and working. Even 95 per cent sounds good, but in reality that means the server could be down over eight hours a week, which is not so good when you're wondering why no one's visiting your blog.

Support: Many sites now offer live chat – online messaging – which can be a very effective way to solve problems quickly. But check what hours this is available, particularly if the web host is in a different time zone to you. If there is email or phone support, check what limits, if any, there are as well as any arrangements for users in different countries.

Above: Compare the packages to find the one that's right for you.

User forums: Before you make your final decision go to the user forum. Here you'll get a very quick idea of the reliability of the service and the standard of support. If the web host provider doesn't have a forum, look for one that has.

Domains: You will also need to buy your own domain to host your blog. Many service providers include a free domain, usually for the first year, as part of their web hosting packages. Even if they don't, domain names are relatively inexpensive.

CHOOSING YOUR BLOG APPLICATION

There are several programs for self-hosted blogging, but by far the most popular is WordPress. Whereas most of the others, like MoveableType (www.moveabletype.com), ExpressionEngine (expressionengine.com) and Habari (habariproject.org), are aimed at experienced bloggers or developers, WordPress is for anyone. To make it even easier, many website providers include one-step installation in their packages. If you decide to go with WordPress, check your web host offers this as it is much simpler than having to upload the files yourself, set permissions and so on.

Above: Your web host may offer you a free domain name as part of the package.

Installing Your Blog Application

Once you have your account set up, you can log into your control panel, using the instructions sent by your web host. The precise method will depend on your web host, but typically will involve going to the One-Click Install, Software Scripts or similarly named section. Select WordPress and click the Installation button.

- Select the domain where you want to install your blog, from the drop-down list. You should make sure there are no files there already.

- Select the database that will store all your content – text, photos, audio and video. As this is a new installation it's easiest to go with Automatically Create Database.

- Some web hosts offer the option of a Deluxe Install, which adds free themes, standard plug-ins and ensures your blog is secure.

Above: Install the blog application by following the instructions on-screen.

- When you click the Install or Complete button, installation begins automatically. Once finished, you'll see a link to your new blog as well as your login and password information. Although this is emailed to you it's also a good idea to write it down.

- Follow the link to view your site and you can see your new blog, which uses the default theme. To start making it your own, follow the emailed instructions or click the Log In link under the Meta heading in your new blog.

MANAGING YOUR BLOG

When you log in you're taken to the dashboard. In the centre are various boxes – modules – that give an overview of activity on the site. For instance, Right Now gives a tally of all your content and comments, including how many, if any, are waiting for approval. The most recent comments can be seen underneath and so on. On the left is the main navigation bar through which you access the other settings.

Above: The Dashboard is the beating heart of your blog.

YOUR PROFILE

Sound familiar? The Your Profile link is in the Users section of the navigation bar. WordPress allows you to have many users to manage the blog. Select in this section what they can do. The choice ranges from administering the blog as you do, editing posts but not making other site changes, or simply contributing posts. In the Your Profile section you can add some details about yourself, such as a potted biography, what name is displayed publicly and so on.

SETTINGS

Click on this link to expand the box and see the various settings you can change. When you've finished, don't forget to click the Save Changes button or they won't be saved.

General Settings

The important options here are the Site Title and the Tagline, the few words that follow your blog's name to describe what it is about. You can also set how time and dates are displayed, which is important as most blogs are arranged chronologically.

Writing Settings

Here you set the default category used for

> # Hot Tip
> Don't select the first check box in your Profile, marked Visual Editor. If you do you'll hide the text box with the WYSIWYG – What You See Is What You Get – editor, which makes writing a post as simple as using a word processor.

your posts and links as well as take advantage of two rather technical features that do make it easy to post to your blog when you are away from your computer.

⟳ **Press This**: This is a bookmarklet that you add to your web browser. When you see something interesting on a web page, like a quote, or image or video on a web page, click Press This and it will clip it. You can then save it, add your own thoughts and then publish it to your blog.

⟳ **Remote Publishing**: Although it's disabled by default, ticking the box beside XML-RPC lets you use apps on your smartphone, tablet or PC to post to your blog without having to log in directly through your browser.

Reading Settings

Misleadingly named, this is where you choose what sort of site you want. Select Your latest posts for Front page displays and you have a traditional blog, with the posts appearing in the order they were published. If you go for A static page it is more like a web site, where little of the front page content changes. If you choose this option, select which page to display on the front from the drop-down list.

This section also lets you choose the maximum number of posts to have on your blog pages.

Discussion Settings

This determines how comments are handled on your blog, by default. They can be changed for individual posts. Select whether to allow comments and if you want to moderate them, only those from a new user, or just those that feature likely spam words.

Above: Reading Settings let you choose the layout for your front page.

Media Settings

For the design of your site you may not want photos in the posts to be too big. In the media section you can set limits.

Privacy Settings

The choice here is whether you want to make your blog visible to search engines or not. The likelihood is you do. To attract as much traffic as possible to your blog, select the Allow search engines to index this site option.

Permalinks Settings

These seem complicated, at first. Permalinks are the permanent URLs for individual posts. The default is to have the post number but this is not a good option if you want your posts to be picked up by search engines. Use the Post name option, which has the post title with its keywords in the URL, and you stand a lot better chance.

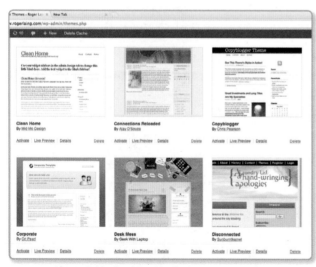

Above: Select the theme that best sums up the feel you want to give your blog.

YOUR BLOG, YOUR WAY

The choice of themes is immense with WordPress. It comes with a number of free options and you can access thousands more free and paid-for themes.

Themes

To install a new theme simply click on Appearance, Themes and then select the Install Themes tab. Now you can search for themes that fit certain criteria, such as number of columns, colours, features and so on. To change the look of your blog click Manage Themes. Choose a theme and click Live Preview to see how your blog would look. Once you're happy, click Activate and the change is made.

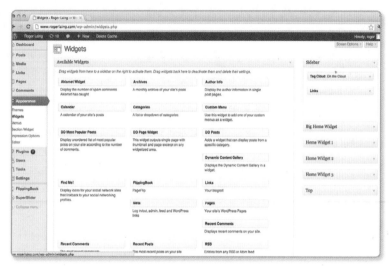

Above: Widgets are mini-apps that will enrich your blog.

Widgets

Notice those nifty little features down the side of someone's blog, such as a calendar of their posts, a message box, or their Twitter feed? These are widgets, mini-apps that you can drag and drop onto your WordPress layout. Typically they go on the sidebar or at the bottom of the page. Go to the Widgets link in the Appearance section, choose one you want and drag it into position. Once you've added a widget, click to configure it. To remove it simply drag it back to the centre of the page.

Plug-ins

While you can add smaller features direct to the page through widgets, there are scripts that will add a range of more advanced features across your blog. These are called plug-ins. They range from anti-spam programs to creating photo galleries or adding forms to your site.

To find new plug-ins go to Plugins and click Add New. Put a keyword(s) in the search box or use the links to see what's popular, newest and so on. The star rating next to the plug-in gives you some idea of how useful other WordPress users have found it. When you have chosen one then click Install Now.

CREATING A POST

Creating a post is simple with WordPress. If it's a thought you want to jot down rapidly before you forget, use QuickPress on the right-hand side of the dashboard.

→ Write the title, add the text, a photo if you want, then tag it (these are the keywords that describe what the story's about that helps with search engine optimization) and save it as a draft or publish it.

→ The same steps are involved if you publish a post through the Posts section but there are additional options. Select Add New in the Posts section and add the title. As the text box has the visual editor you can embolden text, put it in italics and so on. As it's What You See Is What You Get (WYSIWYG) the changes are displayed as they are made.

→ Scroll down the page to set the other options. These include having an excerpt, allowing comments, changing the author and more.

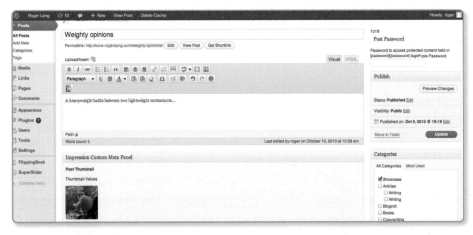

Above: In WordPress you can change font size and format of your post, as well as keeping an eye on word count.

ADDING PHOTOS & VIDEOS

When you want to add a photo, click on the Upload/insert media button at the top of the text box. In the pop-up window that opens you can add photos from your computer by dragging them onto the main window or clicking Select Files to browse to where they are. Once uploaded, you'll see a box with a thumbnail of the picture. To edit the photo – change the size, rotate it, etc – click Edit Image. Change the title to something friendlier and more descriptive than a row of numbers. This will also change the URL below.

Hot Tip

Some blog options may be hidden. To see them, click the Show on Screen button and select the ones you want.

- **Alternate Text**: The words that appear when the mouse moves over the image.

- **Caption**: Add this to display on the blog.

- **Alignment**: This determines whether you want the photo to sit to the left or right of the copy or in the middle.

- **Size**: Alters between thumbnail, which you might have at the start of a post, to full size if it's going to stretch across the page.

- **Insert into Post**: Press this once you are happy with all the other settings.

Above: Choose Alternate Text when adding a photo to ensure your image has a user-friendly title.

FORUMS

Forums were the original social media that allowed people all over the world to meet each other virtually and have a conversation. Largely text-based, they are still hugely popular, despite the arrival of the new social networks.

WHAT IS A FORUM?

Forums are online discussion areas. The discussions are often on specific topics and interests, ranging from sports to TV viewing and technology.

TYPES OF FORUM

Some standalone forums do exist but most are built onto websites to add a social element. They cover all the areas that any conversation might, from politics, news and sport to games, jokes and romance.

General Interest

These forums are general in the sense that they cover a wide span of topics and interests, rather than simply being chit chat about nothing in particular. For example, General Chat, the UK General Discussion Forum (www.generalchat.co.uk), breaks down its discussion areas into interests and hobbies. Similarly, while GeneralForum (www.generalforum.com) promises discussions on every topic imaginable, there's a heavy bias towards games as it's also a gaming site.

Hot Tip

Each discussion in a forum is a thread and there can be several threads active at the same time.

Specialist Interest

You name an interest there's a forum for it, from astrology (www.astrologersforum.com) to taekwondo (www.taekwondoforums.com). Many are linked to magazines or websites on the subject and give readers the chance to discuss what they've read or share their experiences. If you're stuck on a bit of DIY, need to fix your car, or the computer has broken down, forums often have the answer.

Above: Forums can provide useful advice and information, as well as specialist interest sites.

Topic-based

Want to get some help on weight loss or even find out what are the most popular topics for discussion? A discussion board search engine, such as boardreader (www.boardreader.com), will tell you, show the trends over the past day, week, or month and let you link through to the forum you choose.

Business-based

There are many business-based forums, particularly related to financial services and retail, where customers can share their experience and knowledge, and make recommendations. The newer social networks have also kept forums as a way of encouraging discussions between members, albeit dressed in a different guise. LinkedIn Answers enables you to pose business-related questions for your connections and others to answer. Equally, you can answer other peoples' questions and raise awareness of your expertise.

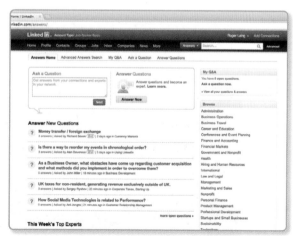

Above: In most forums, the members who provide the most answers are awarded expert status.

HOW TO USE FORUMS

Part of the massive popularity of forums comes from the fact that they are simple to use. Even though there's a wide range of discussion group and bulletin board software used for forums they all work in a fairly similar fashion. Once you've got used to one, it will be easy to use another.

There are three basic types of forum you are likely to come across:

- **Open:** Anyone can browse the site and view the discussion threads without registering. It's also possible to contribute a post anonymously.

- **Partly open:** While anyone can view the posts, visitors have to register with the site to join in the discussion.

- **Private or closed:** You have to be invited to be a member to view the forum and to post to the discussion boards.

STEP BY STEP: JOINING A FORUM

This forum for Generation Z Kids of the 90s (http://generationz.jfbs.net) is typical of most.

1. Go and click the link to Register (*see* Picture 1), read through therules, which are mainly about being well behaved to other members, then click the box to show you agree and Register.

Left: Picture 1: Click Register.

2. On the next screen enter your username. Typically, this will be some made-up name. Unlike social networks it is quite usual to use an alias on a forum.

3. Enter your password and email address and confirm the security code (see Picture 2). Optionally you can also accept email from the forum administrators, which is a good idea in case you make a mistake, or from other members.

Above: Picture 2: Enter your details as prompted.

4. Confirm you agree to the registration terms and want to proceed, then click Submit my registration >>.

5. As you are now registered and logged in you can join the debate (see Picture 3). Take a minute to get used to the forum. As with many forums the general housekeeping topics, news and so on are at the top before you get to the user forums.

Above: Picture 3: You can now post on the forum.

6. Choose your area of interest. Here we're looking at the 90s Shows and Movies and the thread on the last 90s show watched. Click on Add Reply and a text box opens where you can have your say. Like many forums there's a WYSIWYG editor so you can see how your post will look.

Hot Tip

Usually at the bottom of the forum board you can see who else is online, plus other statistics including how many members there are. This is a good indicator of how lively it is.

Most forums offer:

- ➔ **To add a signature**: Usually taken from your registration profile.
- ➔ **Email notification**: When someone else joins the discussion thread, so you don't miss any replies.
- ➔ **Photo/video uploading**: Although there may be size limits. Here the maximum file size is 3 MB.
- ➔ **Preview posts**: So you can be sure how your reply will look before it's published.

MODERATION

You may notice comments from the administrators on some replies. For example, the contributor's signature may have been removed if it included a link to another forum, which is a breach of the rules. This shows it is a moderated forum. In other words, there are checks to make sure people stick to the rules. There are different levels of moderation. On some forums, every post will be checked before it is published. Because the volume of posts can make this too difficult, other sites may only moderate replies by new members. A large number of boards, particularly fan forums, may be self-policing and have no moderation.

Above: Most forums will ask you to agree to their Terms and Rules before you can post.

Dealing With Trolls

On unmoderated forums there is the risk of trolls. These are people who deliberately set out to cause annoyance and offence to other members. This is not the same as someone who radically disagrees with your opinion. If you do find yourself under attack in a discussion with a troll, the best defence is to ignore them. As they feed off attention they'll eventually go away.

CREATE YOUR OWN SOCIAL FORUM

While there are many standalone forums, like Generation Z, they are increasingly becoming part of bigger community websites. These are a mix of forums, blogs, chat and social networking that offer a multitude of ways for members to talk to each other. These are not just communities for you to join – you can just as easily set up your own social forum for your community, however big or small.

> ## Hot Tip
> If you are getting too much trouble with a particular troll, draw it to the attention of other members or ask the administrator of the group – there will be one – to take action.

Where to Begin

One that claims to be The World's Largest Platform for Creating Social Websites™ is Ning (www.ning.com). It is used by the band Radiohead to link with their fans. Fulham Football Club also use it to create a social destination, with a forum where fans can discuss matches and talk about the team's prospects. It now has more than 27,000 discussion topics.

Start Small

You will probably not want to start that big, but there are very modest price plans for up to 150 members, so you can easily set up a social forum for your classroom, community hall, family or small non-profit organization. In addition to the forum, you have built-in integration with other social networks, like Facebook, Twitter and YouTube. It gives you the opportunity to build your community or simply bring all your social conversations together in one place.

Above: Sites such as Ning offer the chance to be part of a growing online community.

SHARING

HOW TO SHARE

Rather than the broad sweep of interests covered by the main social networks, like Facebook, there are communities that focus on sharing a particular type of content, such as videos, images or music.

WHAT TO SHARE

Content communities are like social networks in that users may have a home page from where they can connect with other people who share their interests. They are also able to comment, rate and download shared content.

Above: Podcasts are ideal for sharing content and building a following.

Podcasts

An ordinary podcast is an audio recording that is published online. Unlike radio you don't have to listen to it at the time it's broadcast. You can subscribe (through a RSS feed) so that when there's a new episode, it is downloaded and available for you to listen to, at any time that suits.

Initially, podcasts were little more than audio files used by bloggers to add something extra to their blogs. But they are becoming an increasingly popular way to share content. Many traditional broadcasters, radio stations and the like, such as the BBC, put out podcasts of their programmes. Universities use them for publishing lectures, and businesses often distribute online talks and briefings (webinars) as podcasts. There are also unique programmes, like the Ricky Gervais Show by the British comedian, which set the record in 2006 for most downloaded podcast with more than 250,000 downloads in one month.

Vodcasts

In addition to podcasts of audio recordings there are now vodcasts, or video recordings, that you can create, broadcast and subscribe to. They are also referred to as vlogs or video logs.

Podcast Hosting

Apple, the makers of the iPod, are still among the biggest podcast hosts, through their iTunes store. But there are many other podcast hosts, such as Jellycast (www.jellycast.com) and BlogTalkRadio (www.blogtalkradio.com).

As well as hosting, some sites like PodBean (www.podbean.com) offer social subscribing. This lets you gather all your podcasts in one place and see what others are listening to or viewing.

Hot Tip

The name podcasts comes from mixing the words iPod and broadcasts, as initially they were often listened to on portable media players like the iPod. In fact, they can be played on your computer or most mobile devices.

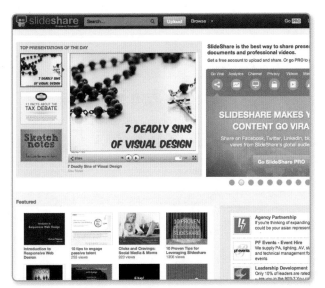

Presentations

Very different to podcasting, SlideShare (www.slideshare.net) is also rapidly emerging as a top content community for business, with more than 60 million visitors a month. It lets you show your ideas and research to a wide audience by sharing documents, presentations or even online seminars.

Left: Some sites allow you to share video content offering tips on topics as varied as tax or web design.

Videos

When it comes to sharing video, YouTube is the world's most popular service. Not only does it allow you to create your own channel, to which people can add their comments, but it also helps your videos spread virally. It's simple to cut and paste YouTube videos directly into blogs or websites, spreading the word, and picture, much wider.

Photos

As natural as showing someone your holiday snaps, it's almost inevitable that you'll end up using an online photo sharing site. Their popularity is such that sites like Flickr are not really one big community but lots of much smaller groups clustered round a common interest. There are, for example, special-interest groups dedicated to photos of graffiti, bands, sports and so on.

Music

The music you like probably spans different genres, which may not be covered by a single radio station. That's the thinking behind music-sharing communities, like Last.fm. Users tag the music they like with a one-word description. You tag the tracks you listen to and can search for music that has been similarly tagged by other users.

HOW TO SHARE

The best way to share content and reach a wider audience is by promoting it through social media, like Facebook, Twitter, Flickr, Google+ and so on.

Right: Sharing content is easy with social media.

Sharing Tools

Whenever you post an update to a content community you should also make sure this is added to your Facebook Timeline or Twitter feed. Where possible, on your blog, website or community page, you should add a share button so that visitors can quickly post to their followers.

Bookmarklets

These make it simple to clip information as you browse the web and post it to various social media accounts.

Links

Integrate feeds from content-sharing communities, like Flickr and YouTube, into your blog. You can have your Flickr photos in the sidebar showing your latest photos or just those with a specific tag.

Above: Richard Branson's blog shows community tools, share tools, bookmarklets and more.

Hot Tip

Once your Top 10 is published you could launch a poll, through Twitter or Facebook, asking your friends and followers to vote on which they think is best and generate more traffic to your site.

You can also use pictures and videos from content-sharing sites to compile a list for your blog post – for example, '10 destinations to visit before I die' from Flickr or '5 funniest dancers' from YouTube. Contact the people with the copyright and get their permission to use them. You could also encourage them to comment on your site and promote the story through their social networks.

YOUTUBE

The arrival of the mobile phone with camera makes it simple to shoot a video, upload it and share it with millions of others in minutes.

SHARING VIDEO

Although YouTube is often thought of as the home of amateur video clips, it offers much more. Now integrated with Google+, this video collection of the weird and wonderful also houses full-length movies, TV shows and streaming events. It is open to all to browse and view but if you want to upload your own video clips and use the social features, such as adding comments or building a playlist, you need to sign up or use your Google account.

TYPES OF VIDEO CONTENT

There are four main types of video content on YouTube.

Above: Create your own fan video, and it could become the most-viewed video of all time.

Personal Video

The spiritual core of YouTube, personal video clips usually recorded by webcam or smartphone camera and of variable quality. They can range from on-camera confessionals to clips of dancing dogs.

Fan Video

Everyone is a fan of something. Show what you are passionate about on YouTube. You could, for example, create your very own video tribute to a star. The most viewed fan video of all time, according to YouTube, is a musical tribute to Harry

Potter, 'The Mysterious Ticking Noise', which has been viewed over 100 million times. It is part of a series by Potter Puppet Pals, which has spawned its own website as well as a tour of America.

Business Video

Many companies put videos of their presentations, demonstrations and events – anything that would typically have an audience – on YouTube. Beyond that they are also creating videos and animated stories about their products and how customers are using them, specifically for YouTube. These are backed by marketing and social campaigns to boost viewing figures.

Above: YouTube has become a great vehicle for businesses to reach their customers.

Curated Video

Where someone has done the hard work for you and screened the hoards of online video to find the best ones and gather them into a playlist. They can be on any topic, from mud wrestling to origami.

Hot Tip

You can be your own curator, creating a playlist of your favourite videos and publishing it to your own video channel.

VIDEO TOOLS

The likelihood is that you will already have all the video tools you need. You can use the webcam on your computer, camera on your smartphone or a inexpensive digital camcorder to shoot the video.

Some Extras

If you're planning to do a talking-head style video with images behind – either still or full motion video – you need a green screen. These are relatively inexpensive and easily available on sites like Amazon. To tidy up the video, add special effects, music, titles and so on you'll need video-editing software, like Adobe Premiere and Apple iMovie. Alternatively, there are tools for customizing videos available on YouTube.

STEP BY STEP: GETTING STARTED

Once you've signed up to YouTube using your Google account, you'll see your profile bar in the top right corner.

1. Click on the downward-pointing arrow and select My Channel.

2. This is where you create your YouTube home page. On the right is your image, showing how you'll look on YouTube.

3. It shows your account name and your bio (taken from your Google profile). You can click Edit to change this. It will take you to Google+ where you can update your information.

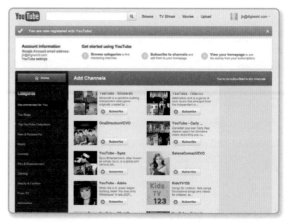

4. Once registered, you come to some suggested Channels (video collections). If you don't like what's proposed, click any in the categories on the left.

Above: You can choose to add channels from the suggestions given once you're registered.

5. Select the Subscribe button to add them to your home page. Once complete, click the blue Home button to view them.

Go For a New Identity

Alternatively, you can adopt a different name or use a company or brand name, just on YouTube.

Hot Tip

When you click to subscribe you can choose to have just new videos shown and to be sent an email when a new one is uploaded.

1. Click the Create a username link at the bottom, then type your chosen name in the box.

2. There's a check to see if the username is available. If it's not, alternatives are suggested. Once you've set your username it can't be changed, so be sure you're happy with it.

3. As it's a social content community, you'll see all sharing activities selected by default. These include adding comments, showing you like a video, marking your favorites and subscribing to a channel. Click in the box to deselect any you don't want. When you're finished click: OK, I'm ready to continue.

4. This is your YouTube Channel page. Time to add some videos. Click the Videos tab under your name on the main title bar and you'll see a few easy ways to add content to your channel. Once you've chosen one of the five options for adding content, the others disappear but you can still access them using the methods below.

STEP BY STEP: CREATE A PLAYLIST
It is simple to create a playlist.

1. Click Video Manager and select the Playlists tab. Select the +New Playlist button, add a title and description in the popup window then click Create playlist. On the right you can see options to make the video public or private, as well as allow others to put your playlist on their blog or show whether they like or dislike it.

2. Now browse through YouTube and, when you find a video you like, click the Add button. In the expanded box choose the playlist to add it to. There's also the option to add a note.

Above: Just click on Create a playlist and follow the instructions to add content to your channel.

Hot Tip

You can upload HD files provided they are no more than 15 minutes long. For longer videos you have to check with Google by clicking the Increase your limit link.

UPLOAD YOUR OWN VIDEO

What about adding your own video to YouTube? It's easy. Click the Upload button at the top of the page. If you have already recorded the video and the file is on your computer, click the button to Select files. Alternatively, just drag and drop your video file anywhere on the YouTube page and it will start uploading.

STEP BY STEP: LIVE RECORDING

Avoid the upload altogether and record your video live from your webcam.

1. In the Upload video files section click the Record from webcam button and you will see a prompt box asking to access your camera and microphone. Click Allow and you're on camera (see Picture 1).

Above: Picture 1: Record video from a webcam.

2. When you're ready click record. If you make a mistake don't worry, just click the red Start Over button to begin the recording again. When you're happy with the result click the blue Upload button.

3. On the Basic Info tab add the Title and Description. Adding tags makes it easier for people interested in that topic to find your video among the millions available on YouTube. As you add a tag, YouTube will suggest other relevant ones.

4. On the right-hand side you can select the Privacy settings:

    • **Public**: Anyone can search for and view the video.

    • **Unlisted**: Anyone who knows the URL can view it, but it won't be publicly listed.

    • **Private**: Only those you choose can see it. A box appears, in which you can add the Google+ circles you want to share it with, plus the names and email addresses of any individuals.

5. Select the category under which your video is best listed. Then choose whether you want to release your video under the Standard YouTube License or the Creative Commons – Attribution. The latter means other users are free to use your clip in their videos. If you see the Creative Commons – Attribution License by someone else's video you can create your own mashup with it, using the video editor (see page 148). Attribution means there will automatically be a credit and link to the video as one of the sources.

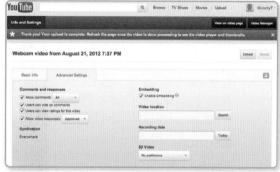

6. Click the Advanced Settings tab and you can choose how to handle comments and responses as well as whether to enable embedding (which lets other users place your video on their blog or website). You can also add details of when and where the video was recorded.

Above: By clicking Enable Embedding, you allow other users to share your video.

7. Click the Save changes button then refresh the page and you will see the video player with thumbnails beside it, together with a summary of video information. This includes the number of views and Likes as well as Dislikes (as you should be open to criticism).

EDITING YOUR VIDEO

Click on View on your video page to see your uploaded video. If it's not perfect, click on the tabs above the player to improve it.

Enhancements

This video editor lets you trim the clip, auto-fix lighting and colour, stabilize the shot if there's camera shake and apply colour effects, such as turning it into a cartoon or changing it to sepia.

> ## Hot Tip
> If you're feeling bashful, or need to obscure someone's identity in the video, click additional features and press the Apply button to Blur All Faces.

Audio

Add a backing track. There are more than 150,000 audio clips to choose from in the box to the right. They range from Chopin's *Nocturnes* to pop classics. Click the Position Audio button and you can choose where to add the new track. You can also mix it with the original audio.

Annotations

This can be anything from a Note to a Speech bubble or Title. The time editor lets you place it exactly.

Captions

You may have to click the drop-down arrow beside Annotations to see this. Adding captions and subtitles means your video can be enjoyed by those with impaired hearing.

Above: You may want to add a transcript for users with impaired hearing.

STEP BY STEP: CREATE YOUR OWN MASHUP

This is remixing video clips that are freely available to use, under the Creative Commons Licence. To get started, go to your Channel, select Video Manager and then the Video Editor tab.

1. Select the tab with Creative Commons logo. These are videos that are free to include in your own videos, provided you credit the source. The attribution is automatically added by YouTube.

2. Either select one of the clips in the main pane or write a keyword in the search box to find videos on that topic.

3. Move it to the dotted line box that says Drag videos here to begin editing. Then add any additional clips beside it.

> ## Hot Tip
> If you are going to include one of your own clips in the mix, click the tab with the video camera icon and drag it into the editing box.

4. Click the music icon, where you can search for the right audio soundtrack. Drag it to the box at the bottom.

5. Select any special transition effects – wipes, fades and so on – from the tab with the two triangles facing each other and position them between the relevant clips.

6. To add a title, click the tab with the lowercase 'a' and drag the title box onto the first clip. In the pop up, write the text you want and preview it in the main window.

Above: It's easy to edit videos and add audio on YouTube.

7. Click Save, give your project a name and select Publish. You might see a message that the video is being processed, which could take a little time, so check back later. When finished it will be added to your Channel.

ARE YOU TRENDING?

When you sign in to YouTube you'll see the home page is customized to you. On the left, beside your picture, are links to your Channel, videos and so on. Underneath are any video channels you are subscribed to, which will show in the central pane.

If you prefer, you can see what's happening across YouTube. Trending will show the most popular videos of the day, with the top videos in selected categories, such as music and entertainment. Click see all for the full list. Browse through and add any you like to your home page by clicking the Subscribe button.

Above: Click on Trending in the left-hand bar of the home page to see the hot clips of the day.

Going Viral

You've probably heard stories of video clips posted on YouTube that have gone viral and become Internet sensations. Sometimes the subject seems unlikely. One of YouTube's most viewed videos of all time is a home-made movie of a baby biting his older brother called, 'Charlie bit my finger – again!'

Passing It On

While you may not be looking for hundreds of millions of views (why not?), you can actively promote your video. You can do so by sharing the link via email or embedding it on your blog. The most effective way is to share your YouTube activity on other social networks, which can be done automatically by activating Autoshare. Select YouTube Settings from the profile bar and then Sharing.

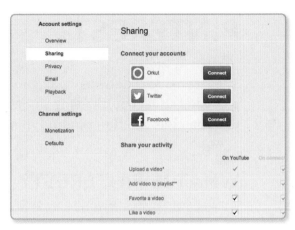

Above: Connect your Facebook and Twitter accounts and AutoShare will update your status when your uploaded video goes live.

KNOW YOUR VIEWERS

YouTube Analytics gives you in-depth information on all those visiting your Channel, as well as stats for each video. You can change the tracking period to find out who has looked recently, in the last week, month and so on. You can also chart how many views there have been over the lifetime of the video on the site.

Performance

Shows how often, within the chosen time period, the video has been viewed, plus changes in the number of subscribers.

Engagement

Tallies up how much social sharing there has been. It looks at the number of Likes, Dislikes and Comments as well as how many people have added it to their Favorites (or removed it).

Demographics

Shows the location of those viewing your video and their gender. It includes information on where most of the traffic to your video link has come from, which could be a link in social media, Google+, search engines and so on.

PINTEREST

The latest social networking phenomenon is a mix of photo sharing site, pinboard, visual bookmarking site and much more, which connects everyone through the beautiful things they find on the web.

WHAT IS PINTEREST?

Rapidly rising through the ranks of the social media sites, Pinterest encourages people to share their interests and be creative. It is addictive. Once people start on Pinterest, many use it daily, which is why businesses see it as a valuable marketing platform. For example, fashion and accessories companies use Pinterest as a shop window where customers can browse before they go to their website to buy.

Above: Based on your choices at registration, Pinterest will select a few boards of topics that might interest you to get you started.

GETTING STARTED

Go to Pinterest (www.pinterest.com) and select the Join Pinterest >> button at the top. The Welcome page shows a range of images and asks you to Click a few things you like. Although it doesn't specifically name the categories, the photos make it clear that it's food, fashion, entertainment and so on. As you click an image, a thumbnail copy appears in a box below. You can choose five boards. Once complete, the Continue button appears. Press this.

Based on these choices, Pinterest selects a few boards to get you started. But first you have to create your account. You can do so via your Facebook or Twitter account or email address. If you use one of your social media accounts

Hot Tip

You can add or remove Pinterest from your Facebook Timeline or Twitter feed. In Pinterest click your username, then Edit Profile. Switch the slider beside the site name to ON if you want to add your pins to your Timeline or Off to remove them.

you will need to authorize Pinterest to access your account so it can post updates to these services. You will also see there's a tick box selected to follow recommended friends who may already be on Pinterest.

FOLLOWING

Your Pinterest feed is filled with a number of pins from suggested users who you are now following. Unlike Facebook where you have to invite people to be friends, on Pinterest you can just follow anyone with the same interests. When they post something new it shows on your feed.

You can follow everything that someone pins by clicking on one of their pins and then clicking the red Follow All button.

Above: Like it? Then click the red Follow button to see more from this user.

⊖   If you want to see who you are following, click your name to view your profile and select Following from the stats bar. There you will see a profile pic of each one, with location details and thumbnails of their latest pins.

⊖   Click the Unfollow button if you think they no longer match your interests. They will not be notified.

Hot Tip

Another way to stop following someone is to click their name under a pin and then click Unfollow on the boards you no longer want to see.

HOW PINTEREST WORKS

Pinterest comes from the words Pin and Interest. What you are doing is pinning images that reflect your interests on a virtual pinboard. Your board is a set of pins, on any topic. It could be the car you drive, your favourite recipes, your Jimmy Choo collection, film posters, anything. There's no limit to the number of pins you can add to a board.

STEP BY STEP: CREATE A BOARD

1. Click the Add+ at the top of the page (*see* Picture 1), then select Create a Board from the pop-up window.

2. Enter the board name, then select a category from the drop-down menu (*see* Picture 2). As you can see there's a range to choose from. If yours doesn't fit in any, select Other.

3. In the Who can pin? section you can add the Pinterest usernames of anyone who you want to help build your board. If there is someone, fill in the box and click the Add button, otherwise press the Create Board.

4. You can change these details at any time, by clicking Edit Board under the board name.

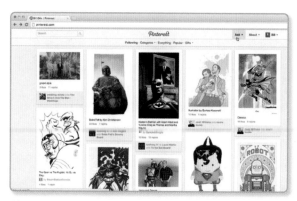

Above: Picture 1: click Add+ to get started.

Above: Picture 2: give your board a name and select a relevant category.

FINDING CONTENT TO PIN

Pins are simply all the things on the web that we tag as beautiful and interesting. Not only do we want to keep them, we also want to share with others who may be equally inspired by them. There are several ways to add pins to a board.

Pin It Bookmarklet

This is installed in your browser (there's also a version that will install on the iPhone). There is a video that shows you how to do this. Go to the About menu and select Pin It Button.

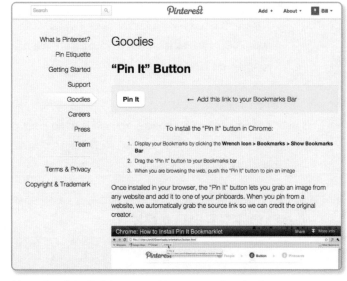

Above: Install the Pin It button to add content to a board easily.

> **Hot Tip**
>
> Notice the Facebook Like button at the top of the board. This enables you to spread the word on other social media channels. When other users press the Like button it will show up on their timeline.

Once installed you can grab an image – or video – from any website and add it to your board. Pinterest automatically adds a link to the site, to credit the original source. In part, this is to protect against the possibility of infringing copyright.

Not everyone is happy to have their work 'pinned'. Pinterest has developed some code that enables site owners to opt out. You may also see that pictures from Flickr and Videos from YouTube and Vimeo automatically add an attribution statement.

When you see an image you want to pin, click the Pin It bookmarklet. This will show all the available images to pin.

⟳ Select the one you like, choose the board where you want to pin it and type a description. If you add a tag, it will help other users find it when searching for similar images. There's also the option to share the pin on Facebook or Twitter.

Repin Someone Else's Pin

Like what you see on someone else's board? You can repin, in the same way as you can retweet a tweet that you think your followers will find interesting. The person who originally posted it, doesn't lose out either. They also get a credit and the source of the image is always shown no matter how often it is repined.

Above: To add to a board, simply select the image you like, and click Pin It.

⟳ To repin, hover your mouse over the image and click the Repin button. In the box that opens you can select, from the dropdown menu, the board where you wish to place it. The original description is included, which you can change.

⟳ Ticking the box beside Facebook or Twitter will automatically share the info to those sites. Click the Pin It button to repin. Note the number next to it, which shows how many other users have done the same.

Search

Another way to look for images to repin is to do a search. Type the keyword that interests you into the Search box on the top bar, such as Film posters. You can then see the Pins, Boards or People with that tag attached.

ADD FEEDBACK

When you hover over a pin there are two other buttons beside repin.

⟳ **Like**: This shows your appreciation of an image. Similar to Facebook, the fact you like it gets shown on your profile, but the image isn't added to your board.

Above: When you Like a pin the fact is added to your profile.

- **Comment**: The best way to get involved with other users is to add your thoughts to their pin. Click the Comment button, add your thoughts in the box that appears at the bottom of the pin and press Comment.

ADD YOUR OWN PIN

Click the Add + button and there are two options.

- **Add a pin**: This is from a web page for which you know the URL.

- **Upload a pin**: Click Choose file and select your image from your computer. Make sure you have the rights to use it. Because of the design of the site, your image can't be wider than 554 pixels.

- **Video pin**: If you're looking to pin a music video, cookery lesson or your daughter's first steps, you can do so. Click the Pin It button installed in your browser when you're on the page with the video you want. Note, however, this may not work with all video sites.

Hot Tip

Other users can also comment on your pins. If you don't like what they say, you can delete it. Simply hover your mouse over the comment on your board and click the x in the top right-hand corner.

YOUR HOME PAGE

Click the red Pinterest logo at the centre of your main page and you can access all the latest pins, in different ways.

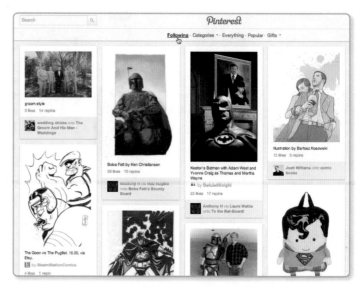

- **Following**: By default it shows your pins and those you are following.

- **Categories**: Select which one interests you from the drop-down menu.

- **Everything**: This, as its name suggests, is all the most recent pins.

Above: You can follow the people who are following your followers.

- **Popular**: As the number of Likes and repins shows, these are the recent pins that have attracted the most attention.

- **Gifts**: Pinterest is a commercial site and here you can see pins showing a range of gifts, in different price brackets. You don't buy from Pinterest itself, but click on the picture to link through to the seller's website.

BUILDING YOUR AUDIENCE

Social sites are one place where it's good to be followed. There are a number of ways you can increase your following.

Hot Tip

If you are getting too many notifications click the menu by your name, select Settings, then Change Email Settings.

→ **Post regularly**: Upload your own content, as well as repin other people's.

→ **Follow more people**: By following people who share your interests you increase the chance that they will follow you back. To find those with similar interests you don't already know, look at the followers of the people you are following.

→ **Comment often**: And repin content, particularly from the popular sites

→ **Encourage people to pin your content**: Put a Pin It button, similar to the social sharing buttons for Facebook and Twitter that people know and use, on your blog or website. You can get the button from the drop-down menu under About.

→ **Link Pinterest to Facebook and Twitter**: So when you add a pin the news spreads. You can also post news of your Pinterest updates on other social media, such as LinkedIn.

Pinterest is keen to let you know when there's any activity involving your boards. They'll email you if someone comments on your pin, likes it, starts following you and so on.

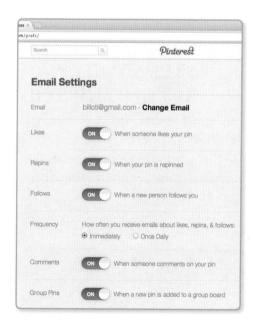

Above: Customize your Email Settings to ensure you're getting the amount of notifications that suits you.

TUMBLR

If you are looking to share content in the quick, impulsive way of Twitter, but with the look and feel of a blog then you want Tumblr. It draws elements from blogs, microblogs and social networks to create its own unique experience.

WHAT IS TUMBLR?

Tumblr posts are short, designed to carry no more than a single image, a snappy quote, brief video or audio clip, or a single thought, and easily shared. There are no comments, but you can like someone else's blog and reblog it yourself.

STEP BY STEP:
SETTING UP YOUR TUMBLR BLOG

Go to www.tumblr.com and click the Sign Up button in the top right-hand corner.

1. Only three things are requested – your email, password and username. If the username is already taken, the box will shake and a message will appear. Try again. Click the Start button.

2. Enter your age and accept the terms and conditions.

3. Enter the anti-spam verification words into the text box and click Done!

4. To get you started, Tumblr asks what you're into. Make your selection.

5. There's a list of suggested blogs to follow. Select the ones you want individually or click Follow All to add the complete list.

Above: Once you're registered, Tumblr will suggest various blogs you can follow.

6. At the next screen you can search Tumblr for contacts who are already members.

7. Finally, give your blog a title and click next. The next screen shows the toolbar for creating new posts as well as showing how the posts of those you are following will look. Press Okay! All done when you're ready to start.

A Dash Round the Dashboard

This is your Tumblr home page, with the stream of posts from the blogs you are following underneath the main toolbar.

Add an Avatar

Before you start socializing with other members, you need to establish your own identity. First add your profile picture – or avatar as it is known.

Above: Customize Tumblr by adding an avatar.

1. Click the +Pick avatar link under the silhouetted picture of a head at the top left of your screen.

2. Select the photo from your computer that you wish to use and click the Choose button.

3. This avatar will also appear on other people's Tumblrs when you press Like and is the image they see when following you.

PERSONALIZE TUMBLR

Click the gear icon at the top of the page and make sure to press the Save button when finished to keep your changes.

Under Dashboard, you can choose to show notifications and to set up a page where people can browse posts you've logged. Especially important is Endless scrolling. If this is selected, posts are effectively in one long roll that you scroll down to read. If you uncheck this box your posts are split into pages. There are about 10 posts per page and you click the Next link at the bottom of each page to move on.

Email notifications let you choose when to receive a message from Tumblr. They can notify you if you have a new follower, there is a new reply or a new message.

CONFIGURE TUMBLR

Click the link to your Tumblr blog and then select blog settings. You can add your portrait photo if you haven't done so already.

○→ **URL**: This is the link to your specific blog, which you can use to promote it on other social media sites.

○→ **Replies**; This is the nearest Tumblr has to comments. Replies allows you to start a conversation with other users. Selecting both options here allows other users to write a response to your posts. It has to be less than 250 characters and will show up under your post.

Above: Click on Blog Settings to configure your Tumblr account.

Ask: Opens the way to one of the more curious features of Tumblr – Questions. It is, in effect, Tumblr's messaging system. A Questions page is set up where people can write a message – or rather pose a question on anything

Hot Tip

If you check the Allow anonymous questions box anyone can pose a question. Unfortunately, it can result in a lot of spam or offensive remarks as the alert box warns. If it does, simply uncheck this setting.

at all. Depending on your preferences, you will receive an email notification when a question has been asked. You can reply in private or publish it as a post. For businesses using Tumblr a page of replies to frequently asked questions (FAQs) from customers is really useful.

Submissions: Allows other people to contribute to your blog. It's not quite the free-for-all it sounds. If you select this option you can create a submissions page with guidelines on what you want, the types of content people can submit and even the tags you want them to use.

Facebook and Twitter section: Gives you the option to automatically publish your posts to these sites.

Above: If the Allow anonymous questions box results in offensive remarks, uncheck the setting.

Directory: Allowing search engines to index your blog is an easy way to encourage more traffic to your blog. If you are going to feature content that's not suitable for general public viewing, you should check the box beside Not safe for work (NSFW).

Hot Tip

In the Appearances section you can choose what information appears on your blog. There are options to show the people you follow, display tags and post album art.

CUSTOMIZE APPEARANCE

Click the Customize theme button with the spanner icon and you can change the look and feel of your blog and even access third-party designs.

↪ Select the Themes button at the top left to open the Themes sidebar. Click the drop-down menu at the top to see all the available options.

↪ Scroll through the list and pick one. In the centre of the page you'll see how your blog would look with that design.

↪ When you are happy with your choice, select the Use button in the top-left corner to apply the theme to your live site.

↪ Rather than change the whole theme, you may only want to change certain elements, such as the header image or title font. To do so, select Appearance in the Customize page and make the modifications you require.

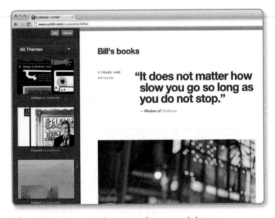

Above: Experiment with various themes and designs until you get the look you're after.

Your Blog, Your Way

Clicking the Advanced link also offers different ways to personalize your blog.

↪ Select from the drop-down box the number of posts to display on a single blog page. As they are generally short posts, the average is quite high – about seven to 10.

When someone clicks a link in your blog they'll move from your site to the new one. If you prefer, you can select the check box Open Links in New Window. Now when someone clicks a link, the page opens in a new browser window and your blog is still accessible.

Select Optimized Mobile Layout so your blog looks its best on a mobile device.

Check Use Descriptive URLs, as this makes it easier for search engines to index your pages.

SHARING IDEAS

When your blog is set up to your liking, start publishing content. Because posts are short it takes no time at all to get going. From the blog dashboard select the toolbar icon for the type of post you want to publish.

Text Posts

Click the text icon, add a title if you want and start typing. There's a formatting toolbar so you can make the text look good. Click the + Upload photo link to add an image from your computer. When you're ready, there are a number of options for publishing the post, by selecting the drop-down menu in the right-hand corner of the Text box:

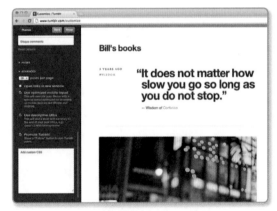

Above: Advanced settings (*see* top left) enable you to optimize your blog so it looks great on a mobile.

Add to queue adds your latest post to a queue of content that will be published according to a schedule you set. It's a good way of stocking up content, so that you can deliver a steady stream of new posts rather than splurge them out, all at once.

Publish on... lets you set the release date.

➔ **Save as draft** lets you come back to finish the post later.

➔ **Private** means no one can read the post without a password.

Further down the panel, checking the box Let people photo reply allows anyone replying to your post to include an image.

Above: While you can publish your post straight away, there are various options for posting it later.

Photo Posts

When you want an image to talk for itself, select the Photo icon. This has more options than the image upload link available with text posts. You can load more than one photo from your computer or an external link. You can also access images direct from your webcam or mobile. You have the option of adding a caption.

Quotes, Links and Chat

Short and to the point, these are easy wins to add to your Tumblr feed.

Hot Tip

Although Tumblr encourages short posts they are not compulsory. The formatting bar includes a feature that will break a long post into separate pages and add a Read More link.

Audio Posts

Music fans will enjoy the chance to upload audio files to their Tumblr. Use search to find a clip you like from Spotify or Soundcloud (soundcloud.com). Hover over the right-hand corner of the selected track and click to get the URL. If you don't already have an account with Spotify, you'll be invited toopen one. You can also upload audio files from your computer, provided you have the rights to share it.

Hot Tip

You can have more than one Tumblr. To create a new blog, click the + icon in a circle at the top of your home page. You can make any additional Tumblrs private, by selecting Password protect this blog.

Video Posts

Again there's the option to add your own videos from your computer or grab a video link from YouTube or Vimeo. You can upload up to five minutes of video (about 50 MB in size) every day.

FIND INTERESTING TUMBLRS

Using the Find blogs link on the Dashboard you can look through different categories to discover more fascinating Tumblrs. Click the Follow button to add it to your feed.

Have a Heart

When you read a post you like, you can show that you appreciate it. Click the grey heart in the top corner and it will turn bright red.

Reblogs

You may want to go further and let other people share a great post you've discovered. You can instantly reblog it, by clicking the button in the top right-hand corner of the post. You can simply reblog the original or add your own thoughts to it before you post it on your feed.

Above: You can show you Heart a post, or can reblog it, by using the icons at the top right of the post.

FLICKR

There's a passion about Flickr that you don't get on all social media sites. Possibly it's the subject, everyone from the casual snapper to the professional photographer seems to get serious about photos. With Flickr you have not only one of the world's largest photo-sharing and hosting services, but also a community of enthusiasts.

WHAT IS FLICKR?

Flickr's ambition is to let you 'share your life in photos'. It makes it simple to upload your photos to one place from different sources – including the web, mobiles and email – and share them through a variety of social media.

Hot Tip

The global nature of Flickr is celebrated by having a home page greeting in a language other than your own, just in case you need to say welcome in Malaysian or Vietnamese.

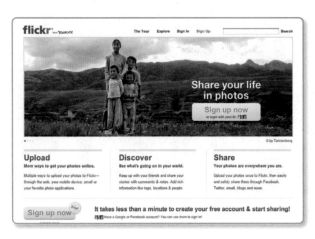

CREATE YOUR ACCOUNT

Owned by Yahoo you can login using your Yahoo ID. If you don't have a Yahoo account create one by clicking the Sign up now button. Alternatively, use your Google or Facebook account to sign in.

Left: It takes less than a minute to set up a free account on Flickr.

STAGE 1: PERSONALIZE YOUR PROFILE

As with most social media sites, the first move is to build your profile. Click the link and follow the wizard through the necessary steps. Skip any you don't want to do. Press the Let's Do It! Button to start.

1. **Create your buddy icon**: This is your profile picture. In the absence of anything else, the default icon is an unflattering square, grey face. The first option, which is to use an image you've uploaded, isn't possible if you've just started on Flickr. Instead, click the Find an image on my computer link, then Choose file to browse for the photo you want (note that it has to be less than 2 MB). Once selected, click the Upload button.

2. **Choose your custom Flickr URL**: This is the web address that takes people direct to your photostream. This makes it easier to share your photos with friends. The format is the same for all: www.flickr.com/photos/xxxx, with you choosing a name, also called an alias, for the end part of the address. This is in fact the name of the folder that will hold your images. Choose the name carefully as it can't be changed later.

3. **Use your username**: Often it's a good idea to use your username, if it's not too long, as this is unique.

4. **Click the Preview button**: If the name you choose is available, there will be a message OK, Lock it in and continue. Otherwise click the link to choose a different alias.

Above: Although you don't have to, it's a good idea to personalize you Flickr profile.

5. **Show and tell**: Some information that tells people a little about you. This includes your relationship status, which comes under the oddly phrased title, Singleness. More typically there's a description box where you can add a short bio, but none of this is compulsory.

6. **Click Next**: Click this when you're ready to move to Stage 2.

STAGE 2: UPLOAD PHOTOS

Flickr are constantly finessing the way photos are uploaded to make it as quick and simple as possible, so the actual steps you go through may differ slightly.

1. **Flickr Uploadr**: This is the main way to upload photos. Click the Upload Photos & Video link on the right-hand side and it will open on screen.

2. **Gather all the photos you want**: Collect these on your desktop and drag and drop them onto the Uploader window. Alternatively, click the big blue Choose photos and videos to upload button (or the Add button in the top left corner) and browse your computer to find the photos you want.

3. **Organizing options**: Once you've selected the photos there are various options to help you organize them.

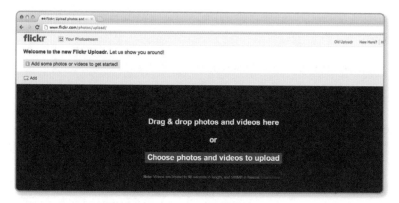

Left: To upload photos, you can either drag and drop a selection or choose the ones you want individually.

4. **Add a description**: This lets you tell a story about the photo, where it was taken, why it's of special interest and so on.

5. **Add tags**: This provides the keywords that make it easier for people to find your photo in a search.

6. **Add people**: This allows you to put a name to other people in your photo, so gradually you'll be able to identify faces across your flickrverse (the site's name for your contacts).

7. **Add to sets**: These are collections of your photos, although you can't call them that as Flickr has coined the term Collections for something else, as you'll see later. Sets are just a way of grouping together photos, from a birthday party, your favourite place and so on.

Hot Tip

If you don't have an existing set in which to include the photo, click the Create a new set button.

8. **Add to groups**: These are communities of other Flickr members who share an interest. As well as uploading your photo to your photostream it will be shared with the Group pool.

9. **Owner settings**: These let you change the privacy settings, such as whether the photo is publicly visible or not, as well as the licence term on which others can use it, if any.

When ready, click the Upload Photo button.

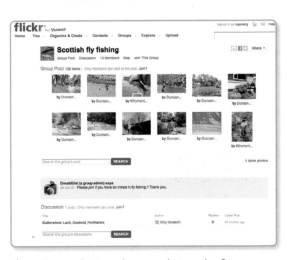

Above: You can choose to share your photos with a Group who have shared interests, such as Scottish fly fishing.

COLLECTIONS

Collections are a paid-for feature. Where a set contains photos, a Collection contains sets (or other Collections). If, for example, you've holidayed several times in Italy you could have a set for each of these trips; and then keep them altogether in a Collection on Italy.

GROUPS

There are Groups of every type, from Scottish fly fishing to skateboarding posters. To find one, go to Groups on your home page and use the search box. When you find one you like click Join? If it's by invitation, you'll need to send a message to the administrator, explaining why you would like to join.

Above: Before setting up a new Group, decide whether you'd like it to be public or private.

Start a Group

If none of the Groups quite match your interest, start your own. It can be public, by invite only or completely private. Note that if you set up a Group as private you can't make it public later. Every Group pools the photos and videos together. In addition, there's a discussion board for talking about your shared passion.

UPLOAD VIDEOS

This follows the same process as photos. There are certain restrictions though. Videos are limited to 90 seconds in length, or 500 MB in file size (or just two uploads a month, totalling only 150 MB if you have the basic, free account)

Make It Brief

Flickr regards videos as 'long photos'. Wedding videos, for example, are usually long, but the good bits, for most people, will be relatively short. By restricting the length of the video clips, Flickr wants to encourage you to edit out the boring bits. You can upload longer videos, but only the first 90 seconds will ever play.

Make It HD

You can upload HD (high definition) videos to a free account, but you will need to upgrade to a paid-for, pro account to view them in HD.

Right: You can view and upload photos on your smartphone or tablet (seen here on an iPhone).

→ **Flickr Desktop Uploadr**: This is a desktop program available for Windows and the Mac. It allows you to manage your photos offline and arrange how they'll display in your photostream.

→ **Flickr mobile**: This lets you view and upload your photos wherever you are using your smartphone or tablet. You also have your own private email address for uploading photos.

→ **Upload direct from photo apps**: There are a number of photo applications, like iPhoto that allow you to upload your images in a batch to Flickr.

PRIVACY

You can set the default privacy level for new photos and uploads in your account preferences. Click your account name then the Privacy & Permissions tab. Scroll down to the Defaults for new uploads section and click edit beside Who will be able to see...

Choose your preferred options for:

→ **Who can see your photostream?** This is anyone (public) or private, restricted to just you, or you and your friends or family.

→ **Who can comment?** As a social site it would be quite limiting if only you could comment. There are options to open the floor to friends and family, contacts or any Flickr member.

⊖ **Who can add notes, tags and people?** This involves the same options as the comments field. The choice recommended by Flickr is to allow only Your Contacts to add notes.

Licence

Click edit in the next field and you can set a default licence for your images. This is only for photos where you have the copyright. You can choose to reserve all rights to yourself, or allow some under the Creative Commons licensing system. There are different options, which allow other Flickr members to use your images commercially or non-commercially, according to your choice. Each one includes attribution, which is a credit to you as the source.

Above: Adding a description to your photo is rather like writing a label in a traditional photo album.

ORGANIZE YOUR PHOTOS

Once you've uploaded your photos you'll want to manage them, which you can with the Organizr. It's an easy way to add information and arrange your photos in a batch, rather than having to do it one by one, although that's possible as well.

⊖ **Add descriptions** along with titles, tags and location information to several photos at once.

⊖ **Create sets and collections** using drag and drop to put photos into sets and then group the sets into collections.

⊖ **Search** all your photos at once and edit them in batches.

STAGE 3: FIND YOUR FRIENDS

Finding people to share your photos with starts with Flickr suggestions, then continues by importing your email contacts or checking if friends from Facebook are also on Flickr.

Share With Other Social Media

Integrating Flickr with Facebook posts a status update when new photos are uploaded. With Twitter you can update at the same time as Flickr and tweet a picture directly from your photostream. For photoblogging, Flickr can post images direct to your blog.

> ## Hot Tip
>
> You can share your photos with someone who isn't a Flickr member. For public photos, cut and paste your photostream URL into an email. For private photos, send a guest pass (secure URL). Go to the photo or set involved and click the Share this button.

EXPLORE

Go beyond your own Flickrverse and there's a whole world of photos to discover.

Galleries

When you see a truly amazing photo, or one that simply grabs your interest, add it to your Gallery. You can build it into your own photo museum on the web and exhibit it through the Explore section on Flickr. Or you can simply build a collection of photos that you want to view again and again.

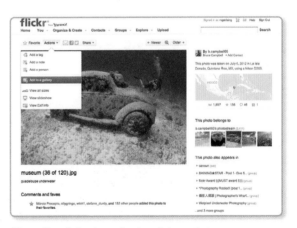

Above: Your Gallery is a collection of photos that you'd like to look at again and again.

When you see a photo to add to your Gallery, go to the Actions menu and click the Add to a gallery option. Equally, if you allow it, your photos may be featured in other people's galleries. You can see who has, by selecting the Galleries With Your Photos tab from the Galleries section.

WIKIS

Crowdwriting sounds like something that shouldn't work but it does, as shown by wikis. These are the ultimate in collaboration, enabling anyone to write, add, edit and comment on the content.

Above: Wikipedia is the largest and most well-known wiki.

WHAT ARE WIKIS?

They are websites that allow people to share the writing and editing of content. These can be almost completely open, like the most famous example, the online encyclopaedia Wikipedia (www.wikipedia.org), or private, where only selected people can work on the pages. In both cases the software allows people to collaborate.

User-edited Content

These user-edited websites are built on wiki software. The wiki engine at the core enables writing and editing collaboration as well as providing the look and feel of the site.

Open-source Software

Not surprisingly, given the collaborative nature of wikis, most of the software used for them is open source. That means it is freely available for people to download and use as they want, although companies may charge for additional features and support.

TYPES OF WIKI

The simplicity and openness of wikis has led to their popularity across the Internet. They allow communities to gather information on the topics important to them and alter them as changes occur.

Company Wikis

As anyone can contribute and there's not one person who has the burden of maintaining content, many companies run wikis for internal communications. They are especially useful for allowing teams to collaborate. Often large technology firms will run wikis for user support as it's quick and easy to update information, and members can contribute their own experiences to help resolve problems.

Personal Wikis

There are also individual or personal wikis – which are useful for journals, project planning, research notes, or pulling together any collection of information. These can run through wiki engines that sit on your desktop, as standalone wikis. Wiki hosts, also called wiki farms, also offer personal wiki plans. Among the best known is Wikia (www.wikia.com), co-founded by Jimmy Wales, the man behind Wikipedia.

Above: Explore Wikia and discover wikis on thousands of different topics.

Community Wikis

Wikia also houses many of the largest community-created wikis, covering video games, entertainment and lifestyle. Among more than 200,000 sites are: a *Star Wars* encyclopedia that anyone can edit; wikis of music lyrics and comics; and Logopedia (logos.wikia.com), which is a collaborative database of logos and corporate branding. You can sign up to collaborate on these public wikis or set up your own.

Wikipedia

There are wikis cropping up all over on different subjects such as food and drink, TV or politics as well as famous sites like Wikipedia. With more than 4 million articles in English alone, it is the free

Hot Tip

To explore the diversity of wikis available there is a wiki search engine at www.wiki.com, while WikiIndex (www.wikiindex.org) covers all things wiki.

encyclopedia that anyone can edit. Go ahead, try for yourself, using the Wikipedia Sandbox to get a feel for how it operates.

MAKING YOUR CONTRIBUTION

The growth of wikis was held back at one time because they used their own language for marking up content, called Wikitext. Now most wikis have the same sort of formatting bar, or What You See Is What You Get (WYSIWYG) editor, that you'll know from writing ordinary documents.

Above: Wikipedia has a sandbox area where you can practise editing a page before trying the real thing.

How to Edit a Wiki

With most wikis you click the edit link to open the page to add your changes. When ready, save the page. In a group wiki, like Wikipedia, your entry will be reviewed by the community. If they accept it, it will stay unchanged. You might find it has been amended in some way, to correct the phrasing or alter the facts. If someone thinks it's completely wrong it may have been removed.

Versions

Wikis keep earlier versions of pages, so that they can be recovered in the event of any problem.

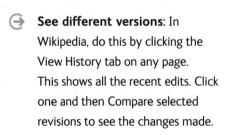 **See different versions**: In Wikipedia, do this by clicking the View History tab on any page. This shows all the recent edits. Click one and then Compare selected revisions to see the changes made.

Hot Tip

Although wikis are largely about sharing text content, most wiki engines allow you to add other files to the pages. In addition to text documents, these generally include photos, audio files and sometimes video clips.

Right: In Wikipedia, it's possible to compare different versions of the same entry.

Undo changes:

To revert to an earlier version click Undo. If there have been a lot of revisions, this might not be possible and the changes will have to be made manually.

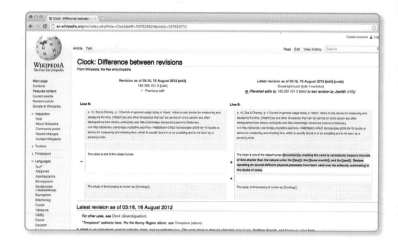

DISPUTES AND PREVENTING PROBLEMS

While some wikis do allow access to all, more often access is restricted to members of a group or community. Within that group anyone can edit a page. This relative free-for-all has led some critics to complain that material on wikis can be misleading, biased and sometimes wrong.

Edit Wars

There is also a phenomenon called edit wars, or reversion wars, where two parties are continually editing the same content and keep reverting to their version. It's particularly seen on pages covering controversial topics. In the end there is usually some form of consensus view that allows the page to be published. If not, it can be moved into editing limbo.

Troll Wars

Because of the public nature of wikis there are worries that Internet trolls and others will target, undermine and vandalize sites, but there are safeguards. If anyone sees a wiki page that has been 'trolled' they can revert back to an earlier version and warn other contributors. Administrators can also block people (or at least their Internet address) from making changes, protect the page temporarily or, in the last resort, delete the whole entry.

80%

91%

DOWN TO BUSINESS

HOW SOCIAL MEDIA CAN HELP YOUR BUSINESS

Social media is changing the way companies promote their products and services to us. In this era of immediacy, it is very powerful, if used well. Used badly, it can just as quickly destroy a brand.

RIGHT HERE, RIGHT NOW

Given that so many of us use social media it's not surprising that businesses have realized it can be a much more effective way of reaching consumers than straightforward advertising.

Many of us, even if we don't do it consciously, block out ads. That's why businesses are using social media, in much the same way individuals are.

Reputation Management

The immediacy of social media provides an instant communication channel with customers. If your systems have crashed, let your customers know that you're doing something about it rather than wait for the flood of tweets from unhappy users, poisoning your reputation. And keep them in the loop. Social media can be instantly updated, so make sure it's used to send out the latest information. After all, no one likes to feel they are being left out of the conversation.

Above: Using social media, businesses can reach consumers directly, promoting awareness of themselves and their brands.

COMMUNICATION

There is a variety of conversations going on in social media.

Business to customer: This may be another business or a consumer. This traditional model of communication is still very powerful – businesses promoting new products and services through online ads, which can be very closely targeted (*see* nanotargeting on page 184). But it has been adapted. Companies are now using the blog or video channel to preview new product features (Apple with the iPad); announce breaking news on Twitter (Lady GaGa tour dates); or launch competitions to tie in with major events (Heineken for the European Cup on Facebook).

Consumer to business: Previously the problem was getting feedback from the consumer. Now you get it whether you want to hear it or not. Like fast-food chain McDonald's, whose social campaign on Twitter to highlight happy customer stories was hijacked by less-satisfied customers.

Consumer to consumer:
Word of mouth has now transferred to review sites, forums and discussion boards. Some retailers take advantage of this by linking their product pages through to independent consumer review sites. They hope to still get a sale, even if it's not the original one the customer planned. By offering a 'second opinion', they hope to be seen as being on the customer's side.

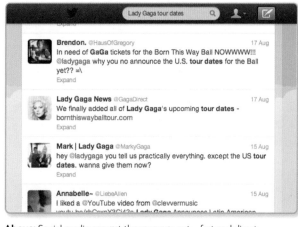

Above: Social media can get the message out – fast and direct.

The Everywhere Internet

The growing number of mobile devices, from the smartphone to the tablet, mean that we spend much more of our time online. We are as likely to be influenced by those we follow online, as we are by family and friends. If you belong to any group or forum you'll pretty soon get someone – or it may be you – asking for advice. It can range from why don't fashion

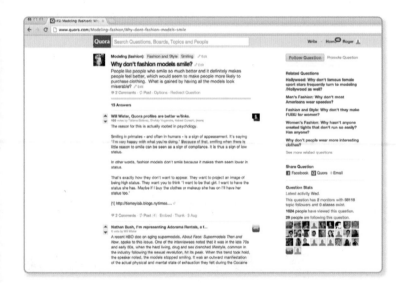

models smile to do you need specialized insurance to cover art books? In the past it would have taken days to find out. Now all that's needed is a quick tweet, Facebook update or a question to a network like Quora or LinkedIn and you have the answer.

Left: Have a question? Have it answered almost instantly by using sites like Quora.

NANOTARGETING

Social media marketing can be more fine-tuned than any other platform. With traditional marketing campaigns you can use radio and TV to hit a particular demographic, but it's not very exact.

Find Your Universe

Through nanotargeting, social media can reach the audience you're looking for, whether it's one person or a million. Through the information users give, social media sites can match the ad to those who are most likely to respond. Let's say, for example, that you're selling guitar plectrums decorated in the colours of different universities. Using the nanotargeting capabilities of Facebook ads you could reach the relevant universe of students who mention guitar playing in their profile.

GOOD TO TALK, BETTER TO LISTEN

The great part of a conversation is listening to what other people think, as well as offering your own ideas. For businesses that can be invaluable. Using keywords related to your products, services or brand, you can see what people are saying about them; more particularly you can pick up talk about features that aren't working well or capabilities that customers want added.

PAY BY RESULTS

If you decide to advertise on social media sites, most businesses use the pay-per-click model. You only pay when someone is interested enough to click on your ad. If that click takes them through to an ecommerce site where they can buy the goods (like

Above: Social media marketing is relatively low cost; the main expense is your time.

the plectrum example earlier), you have a much higher chance of converting their interest into a sale. And all for a relatively low cost per click. Compare that with more traditional direct marketing costs of producing and printing a brochure, buying a list of prospective customers, and sending out the mailshot.

MAKING SOCIAL MEDIA WORK FOR YOUR BUSINESS

Social media has an influence that every business can benefit from, but it takes more than just the odd tweet. To build your business or brand online you need to consider which networks will be most effective, how best to establish a presence and what content to post.

BUSINESS ON FACEBOOK

Even if you have your own personal Facebook page, you'll want to keep it just that, personal. Promoting your business doesn't sit comfortably with details of Gran's operation or a friend's new girlfriend.

FACEBOOK PAGES

These provide a way for businesses to communicate with potential customers so they can learn about their products and services.

Above: It's easy to set up a Facebook page for business so communication becomes a two-way thing.

→ To get started go to www.facebook.com and click the Create a page for a celebrity, band or business.

→ As you'll see there are several types of business or fan pages as they are also known. They cover small businesses, large institutions, products and brands, causes or communities, entertainment and artists, bands or public figures.

→ Select the one that's closest, then choose the category that best fits your business from the list in the drop-down menu. Supply the other details, agree to Facebook's terms and click the Get started button.

BUSINESS TIMELINE

What follows is very similar to setting up your personal account, as business pages also follow Facebook's Timeline concept.

→ **Timeline cover photo**: This can't be an advert, have any prices or a call to action. The inset profile picture can be a logo or product image.

→ **About section**: Add a description of your company in up to 155 characters. The place for the company history is elsewhere.

→ **Post**: Add a story to your timeline. You'll notice that it's set to Public viewing by default.

→ **Milestones**: These have to start with when your company was founded but after that it can be anything from a new product launch to your first sale or industry award.

It is up to you how complete your profile is. Remember, fans have to get something from visiting your page, especially if you want them to Like it.

GETTING BRAND RECOGNITION

Likes are the trading currency for business pages. You need more than 30 to turn on Insights, which is a basic form of analytics that tracks activity on your page.

→ **Like your page**: If someone likes your page they're also agreeing to receive updates in their feeds. Their name will appear as supporters of any ad you create, when it appears on their friends' pages.

➔ **Encouraging Likes:** This starts with something as simple as a starter message – news about your company, tips on a product, a training video or something that can be promoted both across Facebook and other social media, like Twitter.

Above: You can track the number of Likes your page receives by going to the Admin panel.

➔ **Build Audience:** Under the Build Audience menu at the top of the page, you can invite email contacts. Create a personalized web address for your Facebook page; use this in emails to friends and family encouraging them to Like your page.

Like for Like

Just as you can use Likes to track activity on your pages, so you can use them to check on how well other businesses are engaging with their customers.

➔ **Likes box:** Go to the business page you are interested in and click on the Likes box under the Cover photo. In this you will see the total number of Likes.

➔ **People Talking About This:** This shows the number of unique users who have created a story about that page in the last week. A story in Facebook is anything that appears on the News Feed: a post, a Like, share, comment, photo tag or check-in.

Likes can be misleading: As only unique users are registered, if a fan visits a page several times in a week, writing different posts and adding comments, that will only register as one hit.

For your eyes only: As the page owner, you get a People Talking About This count for individual posts that's only visible to you. This shows the number of users that have generated a story by liking, sharing or commenting on the content.

Above: Page Insights give various stats about page activity, including the most popular week, the main location of users and the largest age group of users.

ADVERTISING ON FACEBOOK

One of the simplest ways of getting people to your page is by advertising. Done correctly, it doesn't need to cost a lot of money because, as with pay per click, you're effectively paying by result.

Facebook allows you to target your ads very precisely, based on users' gender, age, location, interests, or combination of these. You can also target fans, friends of fans or even users who have certain words in their profile.

To get started go to the Build Audience tab and select Create an advert. Choose your destination, which can be your Facebook page or your website if you're planning to sell something.

Choose whether to promote your business page in general or a specific post within the page.

facebook   Settings | Log out

Advertise on Facebook

Set Up Your Advert or Sponsored Story   Learn More About Advertising

Choose a Facebook destination or enter a URL:	WritersConvention ✕	[?]	**Get started**
	WritersConvention Page – Website		Start by choosing something to advertise. You can choose any of the following from the left side.
			▪ URLs, *e.g.* nytimes.com
What do you want to promote?	○ WritersConvention	[?]	▪ Pages, *e.g.* WritersConvention ▪ Applications ▪ Events ▪ Places
	○ A specific post on WritersConvention	[?]	▪ Domains ▪ Facebook URLs, *e.g.* facebook.com/pages/WritersC…

Above: Decide what you want to push in the ad. Is it just your page or something more tangible: a product, special offer or event?

➔ Now decide whether you want an advert about your page or to show stories about people liking your page to their friends.

➔ Write your ad, including headline, add an image and choose where anyone clicking the ad will land. Typically this will be your Timeline.

> # Hot Tip
> As you make each choice you'll see the effect on the right, where there's a preview of the ad plus a figure for the potential audience.

Choosing Your Audience

➔ **Location**: If yours is a local business, this can be as specific as a postcode.

➔ **Age and gender**: Put in the range of those you want to target.

➔ **Precise interests**: To target people who mention this interest in their Timeline in some way. Putting a hashtag before the keyword opens it up to similar interests. For example, #sailing would reach people interested in dinghy sailing tips.

→ **Broad categories**: For example, water sports, to reach people who mention these on their Timeline.

→ **Connections**: This lets you filter the audience further so the ad is only shown to those who do (or don't) have connections to your page and their friends.

Setting Your Objective

This is what you hope the people who react to your advert will do. If you leave it on Like my page, you will be paying for cost per thousand impressions (CPM). This means you will be charged every time someone sees your advert. Select Click on my advert or sponsored story and users have to do something before you're charged.

Above: The cost-per-click method is likely to bring better results as users have already shown their interest by clicking.

Fill in Campaign Details

Pay particular attention to pricing. You'll see a suggested price in the Per Click (CPC) box. This is the price you'll pay every time someone clicks your ad. It is, in effect, a bid price based on how many other people are competing to reach the same target audience, which is calculated by Facebook.

Fix Your Budget

Setting a campaign budget is important to prevent any nasty surprises. Choose an amount you're comfortable with. Once the charges have reached that limit your ad will no longer be displayed.

Hot Tip

You can choose to pay less than the bid price Facebook suggests but your ad will not appear as frequently and this is likely to affect responses.

Above: Integrate your shopping cart system into Facebook so users can buy off the page, as shown here. Third-party apps can help simplify this.

SELLING ON FACEBOOK

F-commerce as it's known can be done in several ways. The simplest is to show your products on your Facebook page and then redirect users to your site when they're ready to buy. Local businesses can also run check-in deals, where there are special deals for people who come to a store or restaurant, for example, and 'check in' using Facebook (that is, post an update saying where they are and what they're doing, such as 'At Smokey Joe's, having pizza'). Your friends can see where you go and this acts as a sort of personal recommendation.

BUSINESS ON LINKEDIN

LinkedIn is a professional network for companies as much as individuals. Even if you have a personal account you can set up a company page.

Why Have a Company Page?

By interacting with other companies you can also build your profile, spread the word about what you do through your professional network and find partners for your business. Thirdly, if you're recruiting it's a quick and low cost way to find staff.

STEP BY STEP: SET UP YOUR COMPANY PAGE

To set up your business account click the Companies link on the navigation bar, then the Add a Company link.

1. You'll need to give your company email address, free accounts at Gmail and Hotmail won't work. You'll also have to vouch that you have the right to act on behalf of the company to create the page.

2. A verification email will be sent to the address you gave to check it does exist so that you can continue setting up the profile.

3. You can add other people to administer the account with you. The only proviso is that they also have a company email address or are connected to you.

4. Add two logos – the smaller one will appear next to all posts.

5. Company description – The first thing people will see on your page. You should link this to your website or blog, if you have one, to increase traffic.

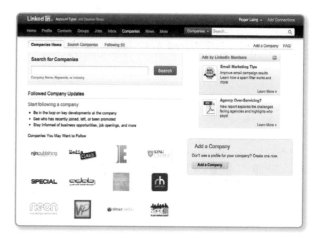

Above: A company page allows you to showcase your business, highlight your products and services.

6. There are a few other details to include, such as company type, size, main industry and operating status. Click Publish to finish.

Now you need to put your message out and grow your follower base. Begin the conversation by sharing updates, posting interesting articles, adding promotions and so on.

PROMOTE YOUR PAGE

You should publicize your page through your personal network on LinkedIn, existing clients and other social media, like Twitter and Facebook.

Adding a LinkedIn Follow button to your blog or website makes it easier for people to connect to your business. You could also include your LinkedIn company page URL on emails and marketing materials. It will be in the form of www.linkedin.com/company/yourcompanyname.

Above: As a LinkedIn member, you can check out stats on companies' employees.

LINKEDIN ADS

As LinkedIn is a business platform, users are more likely to be receptive to advertising. As a result, LinkedIn can be an effective way to acquire new customers. Like most social media sites, it allows you to target a very precise audience, according to industry, location, job role, seniority, gender and so on. Similar to Facebook, ads are available on a cost-per-click (CPC) model or cost-per-thousand-impressions (CPM). You can also limit the campaign spend by setting a daily budget. Once that limit is reached the ad is no longer shown.

SHOWCASE YOUR PRODUCTS AND SERVICES

Use your customer network to get the most powerful selling tool there is – personal recommendation.

- **Setting up a page:** Click the Products & Services tab, then the yellow Add a product or service button to begin. You can add a description, key points, images, sales contacts and display banners for each one.

- **Enlist help:** Ask current clients and those in your network to visit your company page to recommend your products and services: When they recommend you, that news spreads to their network and so the word gets out.

Above: The Products & Services tab allows you to set up special offers and add any promo or training videos you have on YouTube.

- **As administrator:** You can ask for a recommendation by clicking the Request Recommendation link under the product. Start typing your contact's name in the To: box, select them from the list and then click Send message.

- **For contacts outside LinkedIn:** Send them a link to your Products & Services tab.

Hot Tip

The Analytics tab, only visible to administrators of your company page, shows detailed data on your visitors: who your followers are, who is viewing your page and what content they are looking at.

LINKEDIN APPS

While these optional extras are free, they may be linked to services that you have to pay for. For example, Box.net Files makes it easy and simple to add files to your profile that your connections can download. While this is free for personal use, there are fee-based plans if you are using it for a team. There are several apps that are useful for promoting your company.

Above: LinkedIn offers apps that provide added features which will enrich your business's profile, such as Events or Polls

Blog Link and WordPress: For sharing your blog posts on your profile. Visitors can see what you are writing about, which will tempt them to connect to your website to read more.

SlideShare: Lets you display your company's work through presentations.

Portfolio Display: To showcase your creative work.

GROUPS

Groups are LinkedIn's discussion forums focused on specific topics, professions or industries. Join in the conversation and you can not only find out what's happening that may affect your business, but also promote your company, its products and events.

Find Groups

Go to the link on the navigation bar:

Your Groups: Based on your professional interests, industry, alumni and work groups.

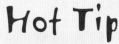

→ **Groups You May Like**: Suggestions based on your profile.

→ **Groups Directory**: Includes a search of all available groups as well as showing some Featured Groups.

Join a Group

Select any you like and click Join Group. A confirmation screen appears. If it's a members-only group you might have to wait to get approval from the group administrator before you can start reading and commenting.

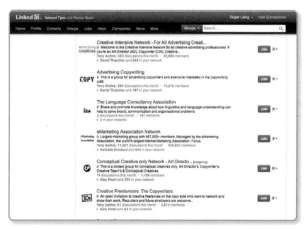

Create a Group

If the right group doesn't exist, you can create your own. To encourage the greatest participation make the group open, rather than members-only.

Above: Groups are LinkedIn's discussion forums focused on specific topics, professions or industries.

Join in the Group

As with any social media you have to provide value to gain value. So don't just lurk in the groups, join in. Post some relevant articles, add some thoughtful comments and engage with the group. Then when you tell people about a new product launch or invite them to an event, you'll get a better response.

Hot Tip

Once you've set up your group, invite your connections to join – and encourage them to invite others.

Use Groups to Extend Your Network

Business is built on relationships and groups give you the opportunity to meet people outside your existing connections. To connect with someone new, go to your group and click on the

Members tab. Hover over the person you want to meet and click on the Invite to connect link. In the invite window you're asked to say how you know them. In this case select Groups and then click Send Invitation.

SHOW YOUR EXPERTISE

LinkedIn Answers is a massive database of business questions and answers shared by users. You can access it through the More link on the navigation bar. Start contributing answers in your area of knowledge and you'll earn recognition for your expertise, which can attract more interest in your company.

Above: Search for specific or industry-related events by entering the relevant keywords in the Search Events box.

EVENTS

Events can be a great way to meet others in your industry, with a view to collaboration in the future or just to see what new developments there are. To find out what events are planned, go to the More link and select Events in the Your Applications panel.

Create an Event

Alternatively, you may want to run your own live or virtual event. To create an event on LinkedIn go to More at the top of the home page and select Events, then click Add an Event. Enter the information then click Publish Event.

BUSINESS ON TWITTER

There are plenty of interesting people to follow on Twitter, so how do you get people to follow your business, buy your product or adopt your cause? Getting some sort of engagement from your followers is difficult and time-consuming. The key, as in all social media, is for you to offer value first, in order to get something in return.

Follow the Leaders

On Twitter you can follow people without them following you, so that's where to start. Use search to identify people who are tweeting about the sort of products you sell, have similar interests, or are well known in your industry.

Start retweeting them. If they're not following you, ask questions or involve them in the conversation by including their @username in your tweets. Like any conversation, if you're interesting, timely and can add a dash of humour, people will want to listen, so you might find they follow you back.

Brand Development

You can learn by listening. If they are your competitors, see what they are doing; discover what they think are the market trends. If they are clients or prospective customers, their feedback can tell you what your products are missing or the strengths on which you need to concentrate.

GOING LOCAL

If you're a local business you're probably looking for trade in your area. (There are exceptions – a neighbourhood art store may be quite happy to sell globally while the nearby deli may not be equipped to ship its goods across town never mind cross-country.) There are sites that can help:

- **Nearby Tweets (nearbytweets.com)**: Similar to Twellow (see page 200), where you can find tweets from local users and businesses.

Above: It's possible to add yourself and your business to Twellow's site, so other users can find you.

➔ **Twellow (twellow.com):** Describes itself as Twitter Yellowpages and locates Twitter users nearby.

➔ **Twitter:** Add your location as the keyword in your search and you'll see tweets that mention it. Click on the People tab and you'll see all those that include the location in their profile. Click the follow button for any that interest you.

Sharing an Interest

Other sites that help you connect with the right people to promote your business include:

Above: Check out Listorious to see what's trending in different categories, like Food here, and who are the top people tagged.

➔ **Who to follow:** Twitter's Advanced Search is not easily found. Enter a search term, then click the gear icon in the corner and select Advanced Search. This lets you use any combination of keywords to look for people with similar interests. You can also restrict the search to people tweeting within a certain radius (from 1 to 1,000 miles) of a place.

➔ **Listorious (listorious.com):** This has a list on virtually everything.

➔ **WeFollow (wefollow.com):** By the people behind Digg, this helps you find the people that others recommend.

GOT A COUPON?

Everyone loves a bargain and sites like TwtQpon (twtqpon.com) let you create a coupon for your followers on Twitter. The coupons can be for anything from money off to two products for the price of one. There's great flexibility in the way you can use coupons to encourage more business. You can tweet them to your existing Twitter followers to thank them for their loyalty, offer them as an incentive for following you or promote them through other social media sites, like Facebook and LinkedIn.

Above: With TwtQpon, customers can redeem coupons online, using a unique code, or in store.

QUESTION TIME

Setting up a Twitter poll can be a good way to get feedback, whether it's on your product, brand or industry, while making it interesting for your followers. However fun or serious the quiz, post the answers so that those who responded can see how their replies matched up with the others.

Hot Tip

For a modest monthly fee sites like twtpoll (twtpoll.com) will help you organize unlimited Twitter polls from one business account.

TWITTER PARTIES

If you're looking for a different way to reach your audience, consider throwing a Twitter party. This is an online event where you can meet customers, launch a product, debate some industry trend or simply have a get together of people with similar business interests.

Make a Noise

Announce your event as widely as possible and offer a small incentive for people to attend – it could be a free starter if it's a restaurant opening, signed copies by the author at a book launch, or a discount coupon to use in store for everyone that attends or joins in the conversation.

Choose your Hashtag

The party brings people together by everyone using a shared hashtag (#) on their tweets. The party host – you, if you are the organizer – will promote the hashtag prior to the event – as well as the event itself.

Party Talk

To ensure the biggest audience you should regularly post news about your forthcoming event on your blog, Twitter, Facebook, LinkedIn and the rest. Ask all your contacts, followers, friends and family to do the same.

→ **Create a landing page** on your blog or website where you can add details about the event, who's coming, what their Twitter handles are, their bio and so on.

→ **Have posters in store** if you are in retail and on any marketing material you have, from email to newsletters.

Capture the Chatter

Trying to keep up with a number of people all using the same hashtag can be difficult using your traditional Twitter client. There are aggregators – programs that group your tweets together. Among them are TweetDeck and TweetChat (tweetchat.com).

Left: Aggregators like TweetDeck can help bring some order to a Twitter gathering.

VIRTUAL MEETS REAL WORLD

Tweetups (Twitter meetups) are also a good marketing idea for businesses. Like Twitter parties, they usually have a theme or topic to discuss and often a guest speaker. At Tweetups, Twitter users meet each other in person. Typically, this may be at the company offices or in a coffee shop.

REPUTATION MANAGEMENT

Complaints on Twitter tend to become very loud, very quickly. If you want to prevent issues going viral you need to be monitoring Twitter. There are services that can help you do this and send an alert when there is a problem. How you respond is key. Whether the problem affects only a few customers or many, you should be open about it.

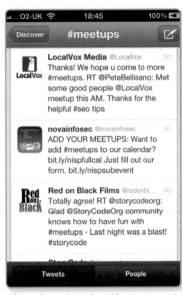

Above: Enter the real world via a tweetup! Rather than communicate with a screen, meet your customers face-to-face.

→ **Publish a tweet complaint**: Be clear about what the problem is and what you are doing about it.

→ **Reply to individual customers directly**: Don't clutter up your Twitter stream.

→ **Show it's a human responding**: Use your name, have a picture of you instead of a company logo and so on.

→ **Use clear, simple language**: Avoid any further confusion.

Hot Tip

Twitter chats are online conversations (using the same hashtag) to discuss a specific topic, rather than to promote a business or brand, which parties aim to do.

Advertising on Twitter

This was originally just for larger companies. They could pay for promoted tweets that were targeted to reach users as they searched or were posted to their Timelines. There were also promoted accounts, where companies wanting to build up their following before a major event or launch could pay to be featured in search results and within the Who to follow section. Similar services are now on offer to smaller businesses.

→ **Promoted accounts**: These help your business connect with new people. You only pay for each new follower you get.

Above: With a Promoted Tweet, there's no ad to write, unlike traditional advertising.

→ **Promoted tweets**: With these, Twitter simply monitors your tweets and puts your best ones in front of those most likely to respond. You only pay when there's some sort of engagement, which could be clicking, retweeting, replying or making it a favourite.

BUSINESS ON OTHER SOCIAL MEDIA

Google+
Businesses especially like hangouts, the video chat service on Google+. In the main though it's the business pages that companies, non-profits and other groups are setting up.

Pages
→ While Google want you to make clear which is your business and which your personal page, you have to set up your individual profile first.

→ Once you've done that you set up your business page by going to the navigation bar and selecting Pages (if it's not visible click More … first).

Pick a category, which is similar to those you'll see on Facebook pages and then add your info, including tagline and photo.

How to Use Pages

Pages let you do many of the things you can as an individual Google+ user.

Add people to circles: This is a good way of avoiding oversharing (flooding people's streams with irrelevant information). By putting your followers into the right circles – customers in one, prospects in another, business partners in a third – you can make sure your message is appropriate for them.

Above: Businesses find that Google+ works for them, particularly the hangouts.

Share things: Post what's new so it appears in your followers' streams. You can lock it so they can't reshare your post and disable comments but this is contrary to your main objective, which is to encourage engagement.

+1 comments and photos: To show you like a particular organisation and start building a conversation.

Create and join hangouts: They can be private, by invite only, or public so anyone can attend. These can be regular, repeat hangouts like the world's longest hangout on social media, or one-offs, such as choosing meals at restaurants if you have food allergies. For a list of hangouts go to gphangouts.com.

Above: Up to 10 people can hold a virtual meeting, or a hangout.

Business Settings

There are some differences between pages and individual profiles. While you can add people to different circles on your page, they have to be followers; that is they have to add your page to their circle before you can add them. The privacy setting is public by default and you can't play games on pages, which is just as well given how distracting they can be.

Ripples

Want to know how far your post is reaching? Look at the Ripples. This is an interactive map showing how a publicly shared post or URL has 'rippled' through the network. To see the Ripples for a public post in your Stream click the drop-down arrow in the top corner and click View Ripples.

BUSINESS ON PINTEREST

Pinboards can work as well for business as individuals. To get the best results you need to optimize your boards and pins so they appear high in the search results, can go viral and spread the word for you.

- **Optimize your boards**: Ensure they are in the right category so they can be easily found. Include a description, with the right keywords.

- **Optimize your pins**: Each one can have a keyword description. Include a hashtag (#) before each one to improve the likelihood of it appearing in search results. There is a limit of three hashtags in any one description. Add prices if you are an ecommerce site.

- **Get engaged**: Particularly with the influential pinners. Don't know who they are? Sites like Zoomsphere (www.zoomsphere.com) will tell you.

What's Your Pinfluence Rating?

If you are more interested in measuring your own interest and popularity try Pinpuff (pinpuff.com). They calculate your Pinfluence rating and will suggest ways of improving it. They also put a monetary value on your pins and the traffic they generate, which you can exchange for exclusive gifts, invites and other goodies through their PinPerks program.

Be Creative

Original pin content will show your expertise and build credibility.

↪ **Add video**: Perhaps a how-to or infographic.

↪ **Run contests**: Maybe for the best slogan under an image of your business or product.

↪ **Invite guest pinners**: Chosen from the top influencers, if possible.

↪ **Offer coupons or event invites**: Give something back to your followers.

↪ **Use pins for product development**: With users able to vote for new features they want with Likes.

Above: Zoomsphere will sort the top interest profiles for your region or country, by followers, likes and pins. You can also see the top sources.

BUSINESS ON YOUTUBE

More than 700 tweets every minute feature a YouTube video link so it is a community worth developing. The good thing is that it's all ready and waiting for you.

Business Channel

With a YouTube channel dedicated to your company or brand you have one home for all your videos, which can be customized to match your company's visual identity. Your channel is created automatically for you when you upload a video.

Build Your Audience

→ **Create your own content**: It's not hard to do and lets you target your message more precisely. Keep it short, less than five minutes and good enough that people will want to share.

Above: Make your board fun and creative to encourage interest.

→ **Choose the right category for your clips**: They are limited, so look at videos by rival companies and see where they place them. You can also see the tags they use.

→ **Send a bulletin**: From your channel page to subscribers. You could tell them about a video you're working on, or include a link to your latest video and request comments or ask them to share it with their subscribers.

Above: Tagging your video increases the chance of it being returned in a search result.

→ **Send a private message**: Send this to someone who you think would like your product, or who could potentially help your business. To do so, go to their channel and click the arrow next to their username. Click the Send Message button and start writing.

→ **Use video responses**: You are on a video-sharing site, use the medium. Leaving a video response will have much more impact. A touch of humour may also help.

→ **Don't forget the call-to-action**: At the end of the video you want viewers to do something – call you, visit your store, go through to your website to find out more. Make sure the final screen has the necessary information, the phone number, location or web link.

Advertising

Naturally it has to be video ads on a video-sharing site. These ads can play before, during or after other videos; as promoted videos in search results or, as they are powered by Google AdWords system, show on the Google Display Network. This is said to reach 89 per cent of the online population.

As with other social media advertising, you can break down the target market by demographics, keywords and so on to get the audience, big or small, that's right for your business.

Pay Per View

You pay once a viewer has chosen to watch your ad and you can set your own budget limits. Analytics, including who is viewing your video and for how long, provide the feedback that can help you improve future ad campaigns.

Hot Tip

Linking your YouTube account to your Google AdWords account makes it easier to select which of your videos to advertise.

Show and Tell

On the basis that the best way to learn is to see how others do it, YouTube has collected together some of the more impressive examples of creative marketing – YouTube Show & Tell (www.youtube.com/user/YTShowandTell)., covering interactive videos, brand channels, home pages, viral hits and creatives' corner.

Right: YouTube Show & Tell is a melting pot of online creative talent.

BUILDING A FOLLOWING

Just as in any conversation, what you say matters just as much as where you say it. In social media marketing, the emphasis has to be on providing customers with something interesting and informative, that's of value, rather than just marketing spiel.

DELIVERING THE CONTENT

Offering promotional content alone is as likely to turn off customers as make them buy. If it's seen as advertising dressed up as content, it will be treated as spam and there's a danger your account will be blocked or deleted. A little bit of promotion is okay, if you provide something interesting with it. If you're a flower shop, for example, it's better to blog about new blooms, which flowers to use for certain events, or the stories behind some of the unusual names, rather than talking about the price of your chrysanthemums.

Above: If customers feel your business is offering something of practical value rather than just products, they are more likely to be loyal to you.

SPREADING THE WORD

The key is to show your knowledge in a practical way rather than just shamelessly promoting it. A typical example is the computer consultant who will mention his qualifications and companies he has worked for, but more importantly has tips on sorting home networking problems. Or there's the DIY store that has a YouTube Channel with videos on how to lay decking or clear a blocked drain.

Imagine if your expertise was linked to a forum on your site where people could ask for help on the fixes they need. You could become the local expert and without, mentioning the fact directly, there's the natural assumption that you have all the materials, products and skills people might need.

BEING SOCIAL

The main trick with social media marketing is to remember it's a conversation. It's easy to get caught up in the whirl of setting up accounts, planning promotions and creating content so that when you go live, there's a feeling of job done. Then someone replies. What are you supposed to do? Answer back, as soon as possible. And look at the other people following them. What are they talking about? Do they have the same interest? Can you draw them into the conversation? The good thing about social media, unlike real-life networking, is that there's room for everyone, no one needs to be left out.

GROUPS

There will inevitably be times when you're too busy to concentrate on creating value-adding content. Join a group and they can help share the load.

LINKING WITH INFLUENCERS

Through social media everyone has influence and you can measure exactly how much influence you have.

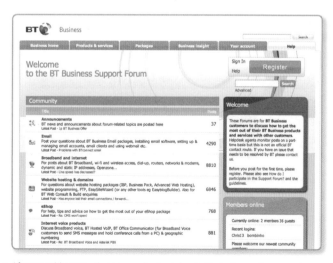

Above: Add some value to your business by starting a forum, for example.

Klout

Sites like Klout (klout.com) measure your influence by the amount of online action you drive. Your Klout score is a number from one to 100. This is measured across different social media: currently there are around 400 different signals from seven major networks, but these are being added to all the time. The signals include:

- **Facebook**: Mentions, Likes, comments, subscribers, friends.
- **Twitter**: Retweets, mentions, List memberships, Followers, Replies.
- **Google+**: Comments, +1s, Reshares.
- **LinkedIn**: Title (as it shows real-world influence), connections, recommendations, comments.
- **Wikipedia**: Page importance (another measure of real-world influence).

Getting Klout

Sign up using your Facebook or Twitter account. You can then link in other social media you use, add friends and finish your profile. You do this by choosing topics you're influential about, which are broad categories like business, blogging, fashion etc, and then select the people who influence you. These will show up in your dashboard along with your score, the people you influence and moments.

Above: Klout will measure and help you improve your online visibility.

Magic Moments

Moments are the main tool Klout has for helping you understand your influence and improve it. A moment is a social media post that has generated some sort of action from your personal network of followers or subscribers.

The best day-to-day moments are shown on the dashboard, or you can see a summary of them on your profile page.

Hot Tip

The average Klout score is 40, so if yours is below that you need to work on your influence. Real-world influence is now taken into account, so your job title on LinkedIn or having a Wikipedia page about your business do count.

What these moments show is who responded to your post, the network it was on and the overall impact of that content on your score.

+K

Every day you log in you receive 10 +K. These are like Google's +1s or Facebook Likes. It is one way you can meet influential people who can help your brand. They will see that you have rewarded them and may reciprocate. To find influencers, simply use the search box at the top of the page to find topics related to your business. There will be a list of the top influencers. You can see the social platform you both belong to and use that to connect to them.

Perks for Influencers

Another way of staying close to top influencers in your area of business is to offer perks. These are exclusive products or experiences that you give to influencers so they can try out your brand for themselves. It could be as simple as a money-off coupon, a free meal in a new restaurant or a weekend loan of a car for a dealership launching a new model.

Above: You use +K to reward people who influence you – just click the Give +K button beside their name.

In accepting the perk there's no obligation on the influencer for them to write about it or comment, they can simply say nothing but you'll hope that, if nothing else, it creates a relationship to build on.

STAYING AHEAD

In addition to joining in the conversation you need to be aware of what others, particularly your customers, are talking about and which platforms they use. By monitoring social networks and your competitors you can stay ahead of the game.

WHAT WORKS?

Analytics tools available on the various social platforms can help you understand your followers and what's most effective when it comes to reaching them. But there are various tools and search engines available that will help you find where your prospective

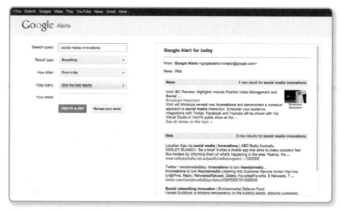

Above: Alerts on Google come by email, at a frequency you choose.

clients are going on the Internet and what interests them. The services below are free but there are also a number of paid-for tools with more advanced features available.

→ **Google alerts (www.google.com/alerts)**: Set these up to track mentions of you, your brands, your products and also your competitors.

→ **Blogs and posts**: Technorati (technorati.com) Google Blog Search (www.google.com/blogsearch) or for local blog search in the US, Bloglines Local (www.bloglines.com).

→ **Twitter**: The Twitter search engine itself (twitter.com/search.), Twinitor, search and monitoring (www.twinitor.com) and Twazzup (www.twazzup.com), which looks at influencers and news stories as well as Twitter.

→ **Forums**: OMGILI (Oh My God I Love IT) (omgili.com) and sister site chatterfinder.com, Boardreader (boardreader.com) is handy to research opinion on brands and searches posts and topics across boards, microblogging, video sites and more.

→ **Social media search engines**: Those on individual sites provide a good entry point, such as Facebook, Twitter, LinkedIn, YouTube and so on. Most require you have an account. To search if you haven't an account use Google.

What Are Your Competitors Doing?

As important as your own plans is your competitors' engagement with social media. There are a number of ways you can keep an eye on them:

→ **Search**: Search Google for your niche. Click through to the sites of the highest ranking and see what keywords they are using to get noticed.

→ **See**: See where they appear in ranking engines: This can provide the metrics and analysis to improve your own position. One ranking engine is Alexa (www.alexa.com).

Look: Look for them on social media See what they are saying, who their followers are and what has gained the most response.

Above: Alexa is a good ranking engine.

Discover: Discover what loyalty programmes, contests, polls, promotions they are running on social media. While you don't want to copy what they're doing, you should be aware of what seems to work for them.

Find out: Find out if they are using social media for customer support. It's a key area where you can make a difference by acting quickly so small problems don't become major issues.

GET EVERYONE INVOLVED

Social media marketing can be very time-consuming. If you have business partners, employees or colleagues who can share the load, all the better. There are of course some sensible precautions to take to make sure that all your careful marketing plans aren't undermined by a foolish tweet or inappropriate blog post. 'Don't do anything stupid' is the approach of BBC News, who have to protect their professional reputation for independence and impartiality, to staff who are using social media for their personal use.

When supporting your brand you need clear guidelines:

Don't put an intern or junior employee on your company account if they're not fully aware of your brand tone of voice.

Emphasize that they are sharing their opinions, not those of the company. This helps establish a more personal feel, which is at the heart of social media.

If someone does make a mistake, which will happen, they should recognize the error, correct it and move on. The glory of social media is that things are easily deleted, even tweets.

Above: Using social media for customer support is a good way to differentiate your business from others.

Dos and Don'ts

Whether it's you or someone else managing your social accounts there are some unwritten rules to follow.

Do: Keep posts short, be friendly and respectful, respond quickly and be open about who you are and your role in the company.

Don't: Make private conversations public, don't forget you represent the company and brand, don't bad mouth competitors and do nothing to shock the audience. You want your brand to be loved. Ultimately your job depends on it.

Hot Tip

Don't forget the average lifetime of a tweet is about 40 minutes, so (usually) the problem will be short-lived.

Above: There's hardly a newspaper, magazine or broadcaster that doesn't strongly promote sharing of their stories via social media buttons.

ADDING SOCIAL TO OLD MEDIA

The conversation in social media marketing has to drive customers and prospects somewhere. That destination is typically the company website, which is evolving to become the social hub for businesses. It will pull in traffic to the blog, customer support forums, videos and so on that are pushed from the social media feeds on Facebook, Twitter, YouTube and the like.

Traditional media is now also being socialized. News is frequently sourced through bloggers and Twitter users, while the grainy images of a YouTube video often feature in stories of major events.

CREATING APPVERTS

Advertising is changing to meet the demands of a more social world. Ads on sites like Facebook are personalized using your friends. These sponsored stories typically show the product or brand logo – anything from a football shirt to breakfast cereals – and a recommendation from your friend.

Social advertising has gone further and fused with applications to create appvertisements. These can just be advertising in mobile applications but the most successful are the apps that only advertise indirectly, while offering a social, engaging and fun experience.

Your Life In an Advert

Among the most celebrated is Intel's 'The Museum of Me' (www.intel.com/museumofme) that runs on Facebook. Subject to your authorization it draws on your posts and followers

Above: The popularity of Intel's 'The Museum of Me' has spread virally on Facebook.

to create a 'visual archive of your social life'. The only advert, apart from the company name in the title, comes at the end. To help it spread virally you can share your virtual gallery on your Facebook timeline.

CROWDSOURCING

Why do something yourself when you can enlist the help of everyone? Crowdsourcing does just that and social media is the ideal way to make the call and co-ordinate the community. Anyone can harness the power of the crowd.

Ask

Have you got a new product or just an idea for one, or no idea at all what to do next? Ask your customers. For example, you have a bakery – what new type of loaf would people like? There are already seed loaves and raisin bread what about a mixed berry loaf? Simply pose the questions on Facebook or Twitter.

Listen

Pay attention to the response and show that you are listening. You may not be as big as Starbucks but you can follow their example. My Starbucks Idea (mystarbucksidea.force.com) is a blog where people can share their ideas and feedback on other suggestions.

Reward the Crowd

Perhaps it's the winner's name in the loaf, e.g. Brenda's Berry Good Bread, or a discount for all who voted, or a taster loaf, etc. You get the idea.

Above: Crowdsourcing is simply getting your network pitching in with ideas, as Starbucks does with My Starbucks Idea.

BUILDING SOCIAL INTO ECOMMERCE

In addition to promoting your business, social media can be used to create and grow your own ecommerce sites.

SOCIAL ECOMMERCE

Online stores like eBay and Amazon are inherently social. They are built around marketplaces, people buying and selling, while taking in suggestions and sharing their likes and dislikes with others.

Amazon

Social ecommerce features include:

- **Reviews and ratings**: Some reviews have been found to be less than impartial, with suggestions of author cliques agreeing to write good reviews for each other and bad ones for rivals. Still, in any community, which Amazon is, these things are eventually sorted out. Witness the fact that several of these critics for hire have been outed.

- **Recommendations and referrals**: Such as Customers Who Bought This Item Also Bought and What Other Items Do Customers Buy After Viewing This Item.

- **Communities and forums**: Where customers can ask questions and share opinions.

- **Sharing**: By email or through Twitter and Facebook.

That's not to mention Public profiles, popularity lists, wish lists and more.

Hot Tip

Think of a trade fair or some local parade where a Twitter party could help you in your social marketing. What would appeal to your customers and what prizes could you offer?

Be an Affiliate

There are widgets to add affiliate links on your blog or website – also known as referral marketing – where you are paid a small percentage of any purchases made by people referred by your site. This is particularly useful for service businesses like writers who could have their own bookstore, musicians who could link to the music store and so on.

eBay

eBay has admitted that at one time they thought social media sites like Facebook and Twitter were just giant announcement boards. That has changed as they have seen how profitable it can be to get socially engaged. The new approach is based on being timely, seeing what's going on in people's lives and talking with them about it.

Love the Memory

For example, for a Valentine's Day promotion the company posted seven videos of people discussing Valentine's gifts and memories on YouTube. They got more than 230,000 views in a month. They backed this up with a Valentine's Day Twitter Chat Party, where everyone joining in used a common hashtag. The eBay fashion team hosted for one hour, the electronics team for another and so on. The party also included a competition with a $1,000 shopping spree prize.

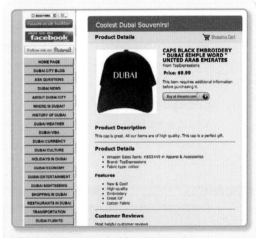

Above: It's very easy to add an Amazon store to your site.

Hot Tip

Add your own Amazon store (aStore) to your blog or website. It takes just a few minutes and no technical knowledge is needed (astore.amazon.co.uk)

INTERESTING WAYS TO PROMOTE YOUR BRAND

Here are some other innovative ways that businesses have used social media to promote their brands and engage with their customers. While it is mainly larger companies that have led the way, the same strategies could easily be adapted to work for any business, however large or small.

Pinterest Lottery

British Midland International Airlines posted several destination boards, containing a number of numbered images that users were asked to repin. A random number was chosen weekly, giving those who repinned the image the chance to win flights.

Instagram

General Electric asked people to snap a jet engine facility and share their photos to Instagram under a common tag. The photos were shown in a special photo gallery on Facebook.

Facebook

A food manufacturer promoted a new flavour of crisp through its Facebook page. Anyone who clicked the Like button could win a case of the product, with one given away every hour.

ECOMMERCE APPS

There are apps that will let you add your ecommerce stores direct to social media sites.

➔ **Set up your own eBay storefront**: This can feature on your Facebook page with Facebook eBay Items app.

Left: Apps like this eBay one will help you set up your own storefront on Facebook.

→ **If you have your own store**: Apps like SocialAppsHQ's (www.facebook.com/socialappshq) eCommerce Tab for Facebook pages lets you sell an unlimited number of products direct from Facebook. It can be set up to increase your fanbase by encouraging people to Like the page in return for exclusive content or using the invite-your-friend feature.

→ **For Facebook shopping**: Hosted platforms, like BigCommerce (www.bigcommerce.com) and Volusion (www.volusion.co.uk) create social stores, in effect product photo galleries on your Facebook pages (or eBay) that link back to the main site to complete the transaction. Other solutions, such as Payvment (www.payvment.com) let users check out from the store without leaving Facebook.

ANYTHING TAKE YOUR FANCY?

The latest in social shopping is a cross between Pinterest, a store, a blog and a wishlist. Like Pinterest when you see something on the web, you Fancy it rather than Pin it. This adds it to your collection. In true social style, you have lists, followers, and those you follow. You can also earn cash by inviting friends, which is in fact credit to spend on whatever takes your fancy.

Above: The Fancy describes itself as a kind of fashion magazine for the blog age.

It's interesting for business as you can buy many of the things on the site. If you have your own online store you can join Fancy (www.thefancy.com) and get exposure as they claim to attract 'trendsetters, savvy shoppers and social media leaders'. You simply fill in a form, offer a special deal for fans and, if enough show interest by fancying a few of your items, Fancy will take care of the rest.

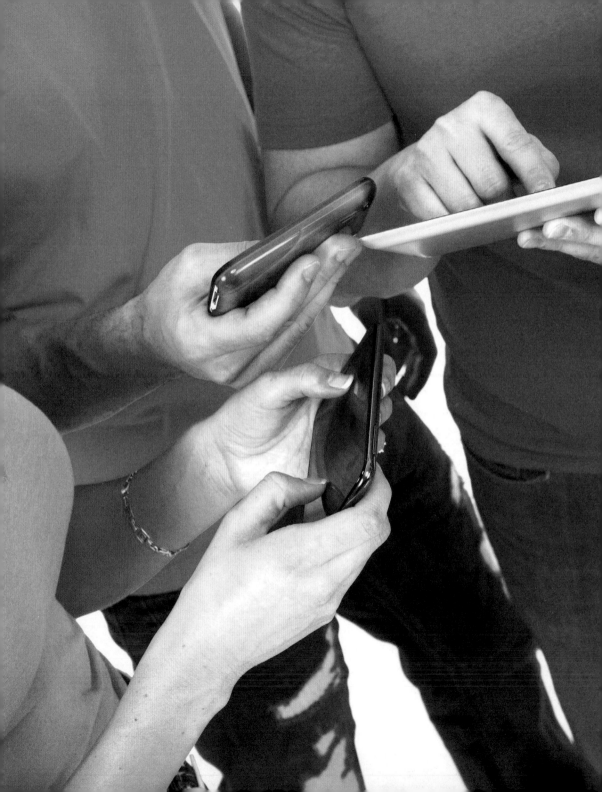

FURTHERING YOUR
SOCIAL NETWORK

SPECIAL-INTEREST SOCIAL MEDIA

While it is the general-interest social networks like Facebook that get all the attention, there are plenty of other sites that cater for special interests, whether that's music, travel or news.

SOCIAL NEWS

Virtually every news publisher, from local paper to international title, makes its content available online. It's usually free, although as publishers look for a commercial model that pays, they are moving to subscriptions to bring in some money.

Recommended Reading

Social news goes further. Like everything social it provides a platform to share what you are reading. You make your recommendations and give your ratings, then it's up to other users to determine if they agree with the value you have given to it. They usually do so by voting. The more popular the story, the more prominent it will be on the site and the longer it will be displayed. On some social news sites you can also add comments with your suggestions.

Digg the News

Social news sites can cover a range of topics, or focus on a specific area, such as politics or technology.

⊙ **Digg (www.digg.com)**: Digg is the best-known general-interest social news site. Digg has human moderators listening in to

Hot Tip

News aggregators, like Google News, will gather together stories on the same topic from a variety of sources and link to them.

Twitter and the rest to see what should be included. A Digg is a thumbs-up, a positive vote for a story, but the Digg score now also includes the number of Facebook shares and tweets for a story.

Above: Some Redditt.com users, redditors, use the site as a personal bookmark collection.

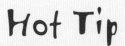 **Reddit (www.reddit.com):** There's no frills in the design but this site is very strong on community, with even the software being open source so anyone can work on it. Any user (redditor) can create a community (called subeddits), which is independent and moderated by volunteers. Next to each redditor's name is a Karma score, which is a measure of the good they have done for the community.

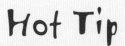 **Slashdot (slashdot.org):** Self-billed as news for nerds, this is the elder statesman of the social news sites. It started back in the nineties and still focuses on science and technology, or 'stuff that matters' as they put it.

SOCIAL BOOKMARKING

When you come across a web page that you like or visit frequently, you can bookmark it (save the address) so you can easily return to it. Social bookmarking is a similar process, except you share your bookmarks with others.

Hot Tip

Publishers are keen for their content to be on social news sites, so often have badges that you can click to post their story to your preferred site.

Instead of your browser storing your bookmarks on your computer, they are stored online, where you can add tags so you can find them more easily in searches, organize and view them. You can choose whether to keep these bookmarks private or share them. Users can comment

Above: Delicious has evolved from simple bookmarking site into a home for all types of content from across the web.

on publicly shared bookmarks and rate them. By browsing different collections, you see what others like and discover new sites.

Get the Picture

Originally, bookmarking sites just contained text-based links. Pinterest and the Fancy, which are partly bookmarking sites, have made them much more visual.

- **Delicious (www.delicious.com):** One of the original bookmarking sites, Delicious is now a collection of virtually anything from across the web, including videos, pictures, tweets and blog posts. Save what you like under different topics and browse through other people's collections to discover passions you share. There are also connectors for Facebook and Twitter that will import links you've included in any post or tweet.

Above: Blinklist is quick, claiming to organize and search your links faster than Google (in 0.18 seconds or less).

- **Blinklist (blinklist.com):** Focuses on speed and the reassurance that you'll never lose a favourite web page again. It saves a local copy for offline viewing as well as keeping the links online so you can view them from any computer. It adds a Blink button to your web browser. Click it and fill in the tags, a description and a rating in the form that opens, then save.

- **Linkroll (www.linkroll.com):** This is a social bookmarking site that describes itself as a free link blogging service. It works differently to the others as it creates a RSS feed of all your bookmarks,

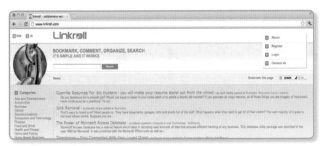

Above: On Linkroll, everything is public, so you can't store your links privately.

so you can access them through a news reader or put them on your own website. It also allows you to subscribe to all the users' bookmarks that interest you.

SOCIAL REVIEWS
Everyone has an opinion and online they can share it through social review sites. These are not professional reviewers or independent experts, simply people like you who have spent their money and are willing to share their experiences. This gives it added credibility.

The Consumer's Voice
Consumer-created content is often archived online, so people can refer to it at any time. It is the good old-fashioned word-of-mouth gone online. Vendors know how important their online reputation is in selling a product (just as it is for you if you sell items on eBay). There has been some criticism that some of the reviews in this consumer-generated media (CGM) are too favourable to vendors and may have been placed or written by them.

Helpfulness Rating
In most of these social reviews sites you have to fill in a profile to be involved. There's no anonymous posting, nastiness is frowned on and the user's answer is rated by others as to how helpful it is. The incentive is that popular reviewers get more prominence in the community, which in turn depends on them continuing to write helpful reviews.

Paid Reviews

There are sites that will pay reviewers – Epinions In America and Ciao in the UK – but these are not the sort of amounts that would be sufficient to influence or change opinions.

Social Review Sites

➔ **Epinions (www.epinions.com):**
A site containing 'unbiased reviews by real people'. Reviewers can earn part of an Income Share Pool. This is part of the site's income that is shared among reviewers based on how often their reviews were used by other readers in making their decision on a purchase.

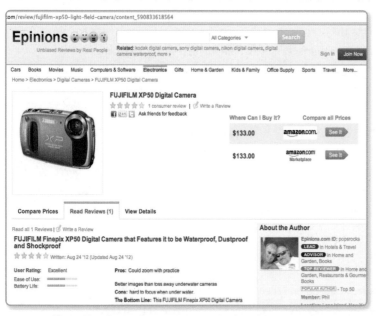

Above: To make sure that opinions are not unbiased: positive and negative reviews are equally rewarded.

➔ **Ciao (www.ciao.co.uk):**
Also rewards reviewers. There's a very small cash payment, currently 0.5–2p for every time a member rates a review as helpful, very helpful or exceptional. In addition, there's a premium fund making payments of £2–£15 that are awarded to particularly high-quality reviews.

TripAdvisor (www.tripadvisor.com):
Although dedicated to a single interest, it claims to be the world's largest travel site. Members can review hotels, holiday rentals, restaurants, bars, attractions and so on. There are sister sites covering cruises, airlines and family vacations.

Above: TripAdvisor is incredibly influential: some businesses claim their livelihoods have been affected by bad reviews.

MUSIC SHARING

Thanks to the iTunes revolution most of us buy our music online, which is fine if you know what you want. You hear a single you like, but what if you want to hear other tracks from that album or an earlier one? A 30-second preview doesn't help much. A subscription to a music streaming service gives you access to the full tracks (millions of them), plus you can hear what your friends are listening to.

Social Music

Nearly three-quarters of us are estimated to be listening to music through a social music site. There are new ones emerging all the time, but among the main players are:

Spotify (www.spotify.com):
The music-streaming service has joined with Facebook so you can share any

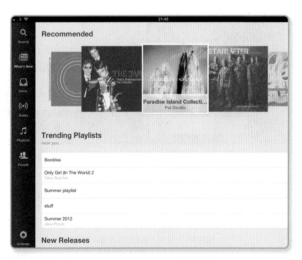

Above: Spotify is an easy way to enjoy and share music with friends, here viewed on an iPad.

music you listen to with your friends on the site. You can see what their favourites are and what they are listening to in real-time.

- ⊙ **Last.fm (www.last.fm)**: This is a music recommendation service. It draws the opinions from your local network and millions of listeners around the world by 'scrobbling'. Although this sounds like the name for a chorus of turkeys, it is a term invented by Last.fm to describe its service.

- ⊙ **Myspace (www.myspace. com)**: Amazingly this was once the world's biggest social network but after rocky times has now reinvented itself to be a 'social entertainment destination'. On your profile stream you can share links, pictures, videos and more with friends and family.

Above: At the heart of the Myspace's new site is free streaming of audio and video content.

- ⊙ **Pandora (www.pandora.com)**: This also links to Facebook so you can listen to your friends' music. Dubbed an intelligent Internet radio service, it will automatically suggest similar tracks when you enter an artist's name or song title. You can accept or reject the suggestion and Pandora will use that feedback to refine its recommendations. Currently, Pandora is only available in the US.

LOCATION-BASED SOCIAL NETWORKS

These are where your online and offline world meet. The idea is that you share with online friends where you physically are in the real world. Then it's easy to meet up if you're in the area. There's a multitude of names for this but some of the more common are geosocial networking, social check in and location sharing.

How Location Sharing Works

Wherever you go during the day, check in with your mobile by posting a location to the site. This way those in your social network know where you are or have been. You can add notes, such as 'had a great pizza here', or 'had to stop at the department store with 50 per cent sale on, just today. Everyone get here!' You can also add a photo and your friends can add their comments.

Hot Tip

With location sharing, you can discover locations that are popular among your network that perhaps you didn't know about or hadn't tried.

Location-based Promotions

Local merchants are now using location sharing to promote their businesses, such as offering special deals or discounts to people who check in with their friends from their bar or shop.

Don't Overshare

Beware of oversharing. Even using the word home in your tweet, sites can pick up your geolocation and work out where you live. If you then check in at a different location they know you're not home. While it's unlikely that a burglar would go to all that trouble when they could just check the house, it's wise to only share location information with trusted friends.

Location-sharing Sites

→ **Foursquare (www.foursquare.com)**: This is designed to help you and your friends find the interesting places that make the most of where you are. You can

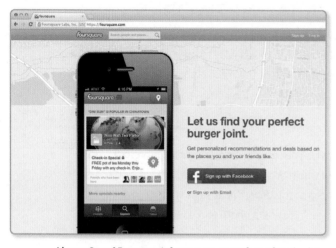

Above: One of Foursquare's features is a view of your friends who have checked in nearby.

Above: SCVNGR has been used to orientate new students around their university campuses and libraries.

log in from the web but it's more useful on mobiles.

- **SCVNGR (scvngr.com)**: This site builds on the fun element and turns it into a game, with challenges to complete at locations for which you earn points and a small reward.

- **Google Latitude (google.com/latitude)**: Part of Google maps, this app lets you stay in touch with family and friends by sharing where you are, so you can see each other on a map. It can also be accessed from your desktop.

- **Facebook and Twitter**: Both let you share your current location on updates.

VIDEO SHARING

The arrival of the high-speed Internet has allowed social networks to evolve from their largely text-based origins to incorporate first photos and now video.

Video Social Networks

Video blogs, also called vBlogs, are replacing written blogs. Increasingly more time is being spent on social video sharing than watching TV. Users upload videos, watch them, rate them and comment on them, sometimes using videos to comment on videos. As well as videos from everyday life, there are professional music videos and news clips from the major broadcasters and other TV programmes.

Social Video Sites

The main video-sharing site is YouTube, with over 4 billion hours of video watched each month. Every day, the equivalent of 500 years of YouTube videos are watched on Facebook alone. There are a number of other video-sharing networks emerging.

⟳ **Vimeo (vimeo.com):** Upload something, watch videos, leave a comment, use the Like button feature similar to Facebook and you'll encourage feedback on your own efforts. You can also follow people and through the forums get involved in new projects. These include the special Vimeo Weekend Projects where Vimeans, as users are known, film a video around a common theme.

⟳ **Daily Motion (www.dailymotion.com):** This video-sharing site has groups and forums and a Facebook comment system. It has also introduced a new micropayment system, Flattr, so that MotionMakers (as video makers are known) can receive small donations from people who like their work.

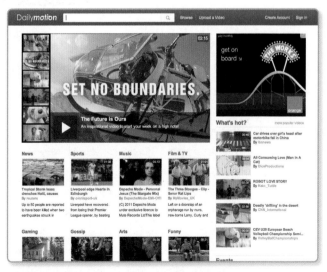

Above: Daily Motion is a very large community, receiving more than 110 million unique monthly visitors.

⟳ **Flixster (www.flixster.com):** This allows users to share ratings on newly released commercial movies, discover new ones and meet others with similar tastes. They have developed a number of apps for the iPhone and Android platform and Google TV, which combine with a digital rights management service UltraViolet, so you can buy TV and movies and stream them to watch on your various mobile devices.

Above: Your activity on Rotten Tomatoes can also be fed back to your Facebook timeline or not, as you prefer.

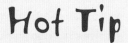 **Rotten Tomatoes (www.rottentomatoes.com):** The sister site to Flixster carries film reviews. It aggregates reviews of professional critics to give a collective rating, which if it passes a certain level is 'Certified Fresh'. As a select Facebook partner, it uses the instant personalization feature. If you are logged in to Facebook you will be greeted with such features as Movies Your Friends Like, Friend Activity and Movie Recommendations For You.

Hot Tip

To turn the personalization off on Rotten Tomatoes, go to Social at the top of the page and select Activity Settings.

SHARED INTERESTS

In the main, social media sites like Facebook and Twitter are used for keeping up with friends and family. But there are other social sites that aim to feed our appetite for sharing interests and discovering new content. Witness the amazing growth of Pinterest, where users can pin images and stories on anything from wallpaper to wellington boots. Similarly StumbleUpon is designed to share with you the things you didn't know you wanted to see.

Shared-interest Communities

That element of delivering the unexpected and following people and content wherever it takes you is at the heart of these smaller shared-interest communities.

Above: As well as finding interesting web pages, Stumbleupon connects you to others with shared interests.

→ **StumbleUpon (www.stumbleupon.com):** Works by getting you to tell them your interests, so that when you click the Stumble! button they can surprise you with something new and relevant. Through the Stumble bar you can give a rating and you help refine the suggestions, so making the surprise greater and more exciting. You can also share your new discovery by posting it to your other social media accounts.

→ **FriendFeed (friendfeed.com):** This is like a real-time commentary on what you and your friends are finding on the web. Like StumbleUpon you can join using one of your other social media accounts. The result is that with a couple of clicks you can share a post with your family or friends. They can comment and you can see what they're saying, in real-time just like a proper conversation.

How FriendFeed Works

FriendFeed is based on a series of RSS feeds, so works across a variety of platforms. As it is owned by Facebook, it ties in particularly well with that site. But you can also read and share via email, your mobile or publish to your website, blog, Twitter and the like.

Hot Tip

Set your Group to private if you want to plan a surprise party for one of the family or want to collaborate on a report with work colleagues.

Finding friends: You can search by name or email address. There are also recommendations of people who are popular with your existing friends. If you want to follow them, go to their feed and select Subscribe.

Above: FriendFeed is available in 10 languages, including Russian, Turkish and Persian.

Creating a collection: Your feed can also pull in everything you've shared on more than 50 other social media services across the Internet, such as Twitter and Flickr.

Join the group: You can also join groups, which are similar to your feed but several people can contribute to it. It can be a group on a particular interest, or a set of people, such as a family group.

VIRTUAL GAMING

Gamers are not always the most sociable of people but now thanks to the Internet they have social gaming sites. Now they can not only play games with other people but also talk about how good they are.

SOCIAL GAMING WEBSITES

Friendster (www.friendster.com): The oldest of the social networks which pioneered many now-standard social media features, such as comment boards and shared photos. It was relaunched as a social discovery and networking platform offering about 50 online games from eight different genres, including role-playing, strategy, simulations card games and so on. It allows you to adopt an avatar to suit your mood, chat with friends during games and use a new virtual currency to purchase games and apps.

Raptr (raptr.com): The personalized newsfeed on Raptr is designed to offer several ways for you to discuss, strategize and comment on the games

Above: The original Friendster was on the first big social networks but has now been reinvented as a social gaming site.

Hot Tip

On Friendster you can earn rewards – points – for different activities, such as adding friends, involving friends in what you do and just for playing a game.

Hot Tip

Many of these games are played through Facebook. When you launch them there's a form that tells you what information the application will gather from your profile.

you play. The conversation can be with your fellow gamers, the game's creators or notable players. Raptr claims to be the only site to support all major gaming platforms and messaging services so you can connect with your friends and the games they play. It has a suggestion engine so you can discover new games and a reward system, so as you increase your player's ranking in a game you can unlock relevant benefits.

SOCIAL GAMES

If there's only so much solitaire you can stand, get involved with social games. As the name suggests they are games that are played with others.

Above: Around 1 in 10 of all Facebook users play the farm simulation game, Farmville.

Some Favourites

Pick up your smartphone or tablet, log in to the games site or Facebook and you can instantly play a game along with other people around the world. Among the most popular and interesting social games are:

→ **Farmville (www.farmville.com):** This simulation game is all about running your own farm. Where it's smart is the way it involves your friends. While you can run your farm and harvest your crops alone, you'll fare much better with your Facebook friends. There's an urban version, CityVille, and there are other apps in the same genre, such as Nightclub City.

Draw Something (omgpop.com/drawsomething): Available as a free app, Draw Something is very simple. You draw something, and the person you're playing with has to guess what it is and draw something for you. It's a turn-based game, which you can take at your own pace although you can get a push notification on your mobile when it's your turn.

Angry Birds (www.angrybirds.com): Another very addictive game with more than 13 million players a month on Facebook. The goal is to exact revenge on greedy pigs that have stolen the birds' eggs and threaten their survival. With the social version you compete with your Facebook friends and give yourself the edge using power-ups, such as Super Seeds to supersize your bird.

Above: On Draw Something, you don't need Leonardo Da Vinci skills, stick figures will be just fine.

Words With Friends (www.wordswithfriends.com): Effectively just Scrabble you can play with any of your friends, anytime.

Texas HoldEm Poker (apps.facebook.com/texas_holdem): Not easy to keep a poker face when you're playing with more than 35 million players.

→ **Mafia Wars (apps.facebook.com/inthemafia):** This Facebook simulator game lets you set up your own crime family – recruiting friends to help you perform 'jobs' and play at being part of the mob.

→ **World of Warcraft (us.battle.net/wow):** It is the social element that has made WoW, as it's known, so successful, you're not fighting the monsters alone you have thousands of others helping. You can change your real-life character for a virtual one, so you can alter your sex, be an elf, whatever.

Above: Playing Mafia Wars gives you the chance to be one of the neighbourhood Sopranos.

→ **Top Eleven be a Football Manager (www.topeleven.com):** In the vogue of fantasy soccer leagues, this one lets you create your own virtual football club. You manage the team, including buying and selling them using a live bidding system, and play the game against friends using Android phones, iPhone or Facebook.

→ **The Sims Social (www.thesimssocial.com):** Lets you create a virtual life – which may or may not run better than reality – with relationships, dating, job hunting, finding the perfect house. What's more extraordinary is that you can play this fake life with your real friends.

→ **SongPop (songpop.fm):** This is a bit like Draw Something for music. Using song clips from your favourite artists or an unfamiliar genre, you can test your music recognition skills. Playing through Facebook you can challenge your friends or set up games with music-loving strangers.

VIRTUAL WORLDS

Virtual worlds are online simulations of the real world. Although they mimic real life, it may be a fantastical environment, with a unicorn as a household pet, or an elaborately detailed cityscape, complete with roads, homes, restaurants and shops.

FEATURES OF A VIRTUAL WORLD

While virtual worlds are vastly different environments, there are certain common characteristics.

→ **Avatar populated:** All virtual worlds use avatars as animated icons to represent you, the user.

→ **Multi-user:** Often massively so, in that the virtual world can support thousands of users online at the same time.

→ **Persistent:** In the technical sense that the world is still there and available, even when you're not using it.

→ **Active:** You're not just a viewer, you can interact with the site, build a home, start a business, hold an event and so on.

→ **Real time:** When you chat to an avatar, there really is someone there, answering back.

ADDING SOCIAL TO THE VIRTUAL

These virtual worlds are by their nature social; they are vibrant online communities. There's also an enormous amount of valuable user-generated content. Users of the best-known virtual world, Second Life, have spent enormous amounts of real-world money to create content for the site, ranging from clothing to in-world games and services.

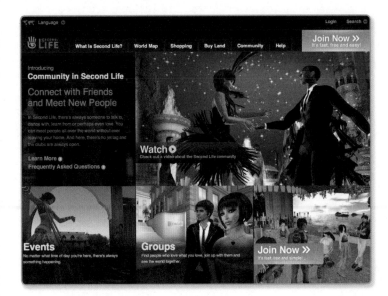

Left: On Second Life, real romantic relationships, flirtations and break-ups go on inside a computer screen.

Hot Tip

Second Life is free to join, and you can enjoy many features without paying anything, so sign up and decide for yourself if this role-playing game is right for you.

SECOND LIFE

A 3D virtual reality that is a game, a playground and a workplace (secondlife.com). There are real companies doing business in this virtual world: clothes designers, artists, builders and service companies all exchanging skills for money (which is a fake currency linked to real ones).

Shifting Reality

→ **Start slow:** Go to the Second Life website and click Your World. The choices start immediately. Select your avatar (graphical representation of you). If you don't want to be a person, you can be a vehicle, robot or vampire.

→ **Open an account:** Create a username, enter a few personal details, before choosing whether you want the basic free account or premium one. With the upgraded account you can build your own private home, access to adult areas and gain virtual rewards and gifts.

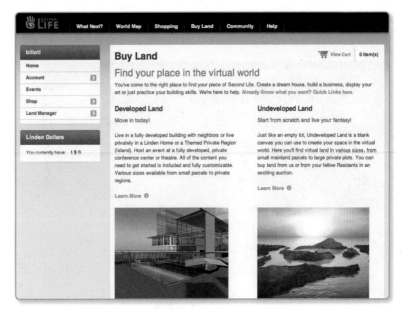

Destinations:
Even with the free account the range of destinations is incredible, covering everything from ancient cities to space stations.

Get started:
With your account activated, download the 3D browsing software to get started.

Above: Second Life allows you build the house of your dreams wherever you like.

How to Play

Log in to Second Life and your brave new inworld, as it's called, opens. This is also referred to as SL by users (as opposed to First Life or FL for the real world). The first time you log in you should see Welcome Island, which gives you a quick tour round the Second Life Viewer and how to use it.

Learn to Walk

You walk in this virtual world by using various key combinations. They also let you change your view, run and fly (only in some regions as the different lands of SL are known) so it's not quite like real life. You can access them from the Move (Walk/Run/Fly) button on the bottom toolbar.

Interacting... With Objects

When your mouse goes over some objects, like furniture, you'll see a sit icon. Click and your avatar does just that. Clicking on objects will usually lead to some action or show a menu with further options.

Left: Part of the fun of Second Life is where you go: choose your destination from various categories.

Interacting... With People

You can find out more about the people near you by putting the mouse over their avatar and clicking the information icon that appears. It has basic bio details and lets you control the voice chat volume with that individual. Click Add friend to invite them to be just that.

Start a Conversation

Click the Chat button on the bottom toolbar and you can also text chat people nearby.

Meet People

The People button opens the People window that has four tabs:

- **Nearby:** everyone within 100 metres.
- **My Friends:** your friends list, with those online shown first.
- **My Groups:** information on the groups – like clubs – you have joined.
- **Recent:** everyone you've been communicating with recently.

Take the time to talk to the people around you. You never know where these friendships may lead and you might end up starting a business together.

Destination Unknown

Click on the Search icon (magnifying glass) and select the Destination Guide. You can either search for a particular place, if you know what you want, or click See all to view a complete list. You could choose Sheepville, a romantic little village, explore ancient Rome or pick up freebies aboard a space station. To get there press the Teleport button. Once you're there, press the Map button and you'll see more details, such as any friends already there.

Above: Once you've decided on your destination, press the Teleport button.

Maturity Rating

Beside each destination you'll find a maturity rating. This is an indication of the level of adult content that might be there.

→ **General:** Nothing sexually explicit or violent and no nudity is depicted.

→ **Moderate:** Covering many areas of Second Life without adult content. There could be a sexy outfit in a shop or a burlesque troupe in a club but not a strip club itself.

Adult: The red light zone, this covers any content that is sexually explicit, intensely violent or depicts illicit drug use. It may surprise you that content like this is allowed, but the argument is that Second Life is a realistic reflection of First Life. Any content in this category has to be on the adult mainland continent, called Zindra, or in a private region that the owner has marked as Adult.

Above: Second Life allows you to buy property using your Linden dollars.

Money

You don't have to have money to enjoy Second Life, but like anything else it is a much richer experience if you do. The currency in Second Life is called the Linden Dollar (L$) and you get these virtual bucks by buying them with real money through the Second Life Exchange. You can then use your dollars to buy just about anything you could in real life, including virtual land on which you can buy exclusive properties, homes, bars or restaurants and resell them like any property developer.

Freebies

To save your dollars you can get stuff for free. There are groups that are dedicated to sharing

Hot Tip

Money does grow on trees. For the first 30 days on Second Life you can pick these Linden dollars up for free. Just search for money tree in the Classifieds or the Places tab.

places where you can get them (search for lucky chairs or dumpster diving), and you can search the classifieds for free stuff in the shopping section.

OTHER VIRTUAL WORLDS

While Second Life is well known, there are other virtual worlds.

Blue Mars (www.bluemars.com): Inside Blue Mars you can explore, connect with friends, go to events, listen to a concert, but it is primarily a development platform for others who want to create their own commercial 3D worlds.

Kaneva (www.kaneva.com): A free 3D virtual world that mirrors the activities of the real world, where you have your own home, can design and sell things and entertain friends.

Habbo Hotel (www.habbo.com): Aimed at teenagers, this virtual hotel plans to improve their social skills while they have fun with friends. Users can build games to challenge their friends, decorate their rooms or dress up their avatars to reflect their personality.

Above: Kaneva combines social networking with a 3D virtual world.

JARGON BUSTER

Affiliate (referral) marketing
You are paid a small percentage for any purchases made by people who were referred by clicking a link on your site.

Aggregators
Websites (like FriendFeed) and software programs that pull content – such as blog posts, news stories, videos, tweets or status updates – from various sources and present them together.

Android
The technology platform created by Google for smartphones and tablets to rival Apple's iPhone and iPad.

App
The short name for the application software that runs a game or program on your computer, smartphone or tablet.

Avatars
Animated characters that represent users in a virtual world.

Blog
Short for weblog, it has gone from meaning a personal online diary to any form of content publishing, particularly where posts are shown chronologically.

Blogosphere
The collective name for all the blogs on the Internet.

Bookmark/Bookmarklet
Saving a web page that you like or visit frequently in your browser so you can easily return to it. A bookmarklet lets you send the link direct to a social bookmarking site.

Browser
The software that lets you view web pages on your computer or mobile device. The best known include Chrome, Firefox, Safari and Internet Explorer.

Crowdsourcing
Enlisting the help of everyone for your project and using social media to organize it.

Ecommerce
The buying and selling of goods and services over the Internet.

Feed (RSS feed)
A method of pulling together and distributing content, also referred to as a RSS (Really Simple Syndication). When you subscribe the content is automatically sent.

Forum
An online discussion board.

Friending
Adding someone to your list of friends or followers.

Hangout
A video chat on Google+.

Hashtag
The tag (#) in a tweet that makes it easy to find all those with the same tag in a search.

Location sharing
Sharing where you physically are in the real world with your online friends.

Also known as geosocial networking and social check in.

Mashup
Mixing together different sources of information to create something new. It can be combining several people's video clips into one, or using map and social networking apps together to create a new location-sharing program.

Microblogging
Like blogging, except the posts are much shorter (140 characters or fewer, including spaces, on Twitter, the best-known example).

MMORPG
Massively Multiplayer Online Role-Playing Game, such as Second Life, if you think it's a game. If not, World of War is another example.

Open source
Software that is open for any developer to contribute to and is freely distributed.

Pay per click (PPC)
Pricing model where advertisers are only charged for the number of times visitors have clicked their ad.

Permalink
The permanent link that is used to open a specific blog post, even when it's in the archive.

Plug-ins
Special scripts that you can add to your blog or other software to add additional features – such as play video or help protect against spam.

Podcast
A regular broadcast over the Internet, usually of an audio file, listened to on your computer or mobile device. The video equivalent is a vodcast.

Post
An entry in a blog or social network.

Search engine
Online directories for finding information on the Internet. The biggest include Google, Bing and Yahoo.

SEO
Search Engine Optimization is a way of increasing the ranking of a website or web page in search engine results.

Smartphone
A mix of phone, media players, video camera, GPS navigation, web browser and much more, in one handheld device.

Spam
Thanks to a Monty Python sketch where this pre-cooked 'spiced ham' meat product was everywhere and inescapable, spam is also the name for unsolicited electronic messages, usually ads, that pop up in email, comments, tweets and so on.

Status update
Similar to a post, it's the name used on some social networks for the message you write to let everyone know what you're doing.

Stream
The name some sites use for the flow of content – posts, audio, video, updates – featured on your home page.

Streaming
This is multimedia, such as a movie, that you watch as it's being downloaded to your computer or mobile device, rather than waiting for it to fully download before viewing.

Tablet
Bigger than a phone, smaller than a laptop, tablet computers are mobile computers that are primarily operated using the touch screen. Best known is the iPad but there are others for the Android and Windows platforms.

Tag
Adding a keyword to content, such as a blogpost, tweet, bookmark, that describes what it's about so that it is easier to find in a search.

Timeline
This way of ordering events and activities chronologically has been adopted by Facebook and other social networks to structure your profile. As well as showing what you have done on the site – and when – you can also add important real-life events.

Trending
The posts, stories or topics that are currently most popular with users.

Trolls
People who deliberately set out to cause annoyance and offence to other members of an online community.

Tweet
A message sent on Twitter, the microblogging service, which has to be 140 characters or fewer.

URL
Uniform Resource Locator. The web address for something, for example http://www.google.com is the URL for Google.

User-generated content
Where the content is produced by the community that consumes it. It can be based around virtually any content, including blogs, social networks, video, forums, photos and news.

Viral
Refers to any content – videos, photos, tweets or games – that becomes massively popular by being shared across the Internet – the 'word of mouth' for the digital age.

Virtual world
A 3D computer environment that simulates real life. It can seek to mimic real life or present a much more fantastical vision. In Second Life, the most famous example of a virtual world, there are both elements.

Widgets
A widget is like a plug-in that you drag and drop to run in certain parts of your blog, normally the side bar.

Wiki
User-edited websites that allow people to share the writing and editing of content. The wiki engine is the software that runs it. A wiki farm is the name for a wiki-hosting service where you can have your personal wiki.

WYSIWYG
Acronym for What You See Is What You Get, a text editor for blogs, wikis and web pages that will display your content on screen exactly as it will look when published online.

FURTHER READING

Brown, Eileen, *Working the Crowd: Social Media Marketing for Business*, British Informatics Society Ltd., 2012.

Clapperton, Guy, *This is Social Media: Tweet, Blog, Link and Post Your Way to Business Success*, Capstone, 2009

Collins, Tim, *The Little Book of Twitter: Get Tweetwise!*, Michael O'Mara Books Ltd., 2009

Kerpen, Dave, *Likeable Social Media: How to Delight Your Customers, Create an Irresistible Brand, and Be Generally Amazing on Facebook (& Other Social Networks)*, McGraw-Hill Professional, 2011.

Safko, Lon, *The Social Media Bible: Tactics, Tools, and Strategies for Business Success*, John Wiley & Sons, 2012.

Zimmerman, Jan and Sahlin, Doug, *Social Media Marketing All-in-One For Dummies*, John Wiley & Sons, 2010.

WEBSITES

www.blogs.com
A service that helps you find blogs by category and topic or read daily blog roundups of some of the best blog content around the web.

www.brandwatch.com
Brandwatch is one of the world's leading tools for monitoring and analysing social media.

chime.in
This is a general social news sites include business, entertainment, sports, health and tech.

delicious.com
A social bookmarking site, which invites users to organize and publicize interesting items through tagging and networking.

digg.com
Allows users to share articles with their friends list or post to the most popular blog sites directly.

www.facebook.com
With over 1 billion active users worldwide, this is the big daddy of social networks, used more and more by business.

www.fark.com
This is a community news site which allows users to comment on news articles.

www.flickr.com
Online photosharing and management.

www.hubspot.com
Hubspot make an inbound marketing software that offers businesses an all-in-one marketing solution.

www.linkedin.com
A networking site where alumni, business associates, recent graduates and other professionals connect online.

www.livejournal.com
This site is part self-publishing network and part blog.

www.mashable.com
Online news site with big emphasis on social media. Also accessible through LinkedIn and Facebook.

www.myspace.com
The re-launched MySpace is similar to a grapevine in that it aggregates opinion from within your networks on what to listen to and what to watch.

www.newsvine.com
This site consists of community-driven news stories and opinions.

pinterest.com
A content-sharing service that allows members to 'pin' images, videos and other objects to their pinboard.

www.readwriteweb.com
Widely read blog providing web technology news, reviews and analysis.

www.redditt.com
A popular social news site with a large user base.

secondlife.com
A 3-D virtual world that is so popular it makes money by selling virtual real-estate for hard cash.

slashdot.org
Slashdot is a tech site to which users can submit stories for possible publication.

www.socialmediaexaminer.com
Claims to be the world's largest online social media magazine helping businesses to best use social media tools like Facebook, Twitter and LinkedIn.

www.stumbleupon.com
StumbleUpon is a social network and browser toolbar which allows users to channel surf the internet.

www.technorati.com
Technorati is a real-time search for user-generated media (including weblogs) by tag or keyword. It also provides popularity indexes.

thenextweb.com/socialmedia
A blog that focuses on international technology news, business and culture.

www.tumblr.com
A free blog-hosting platform offering features such as templates and mobile apps.

twitter.com
Follow your friends, experts, favourite celebrities and breaking news.

venturebeat.com
VentureBeat is a technology blog that focuses on innovative companies and the executives behind them.

wallblog.co.uk
A blog covering digital marketing, digital media, social media, search marketing, ecommerce and email.

wikipedia.org
The world's largest wiki with information on just about everything that you can edit, subject to approval.

www.youtube.com
Watch and share video content.

INDEX